WOMEN'S SURVIVAL GUIDE
FOR OVERCOMING
OBSTACLES,
TRANSITION &
CHANGE

To Olney- My Family's friends!
Karen B Wasserman, PsyD, RN

D1218272

Edited by Linda Ellis Eastman

Professional Woman Publishing
Prospect, Kentucky

WOMEN'S SURVIVAL GUIDE FOR OVERCOMING
OBSTACLES, TRANSITION & CHANGE

Published by:
Professional Woman Publishing
Post Office Box 333
Prospect, KY 40059
(502) 228-0906
http://www.prowoman.net

Please contact the publisher for quantity discounts.

ISBN 13: 978-0-9791153-9-4
ISBN 10: 0-9791153-9-6

Library of Congress Cataloging-In-Publication Data

Cover Design and Typography by:
Sential Design, LLC — www.sentialdesign.com

Printed in the United States of America

For Dorothy Bittmann, a woman of amazing courage and
strength who has faced numerous challenges with dignity and grace.

TABLE OF CONTENTS

TABLE OF CONTENTS
–CONTINUED–

TABLE OF CONTENTS
-CONTINUED-

ABOUT THE AUTHOR

LINDA EASTMAN

Linda Ellis Eastman is President and CEO of The Professional Woman Network (PWN), an International Training and Consulting Organization on Women's Issues. She has designed seminars which have been presented in China, the former Soviet Union, South Africa, the Phillipines, and attended by individuals in the United States from such firms as McDonalds, USA Today, Siemens-Westinghouse, the Pentagon, the Department of Defense, and the United States Department of Education.

An expert on women's issues, Ms. Eastman has certified and trained over one thousand women to start consulting/seminar businesses originating from such countries as Pakistan, the Ukraine, Antigua, Canada, Mexico, Zimbabwe, Nigeria, Bermuda, Jamaica, Costa Rica, England, South Africa, Malaysia, and Kenya. Founded in 1982 by Linda Ellis Eastman, The Professional Woman Network is committed to educating women on a global basis regarding, self-esteem, confidence building, stress management, and emotional, mental, spiritual and physical wellness.

Ms. Eastman has been featured in USA Today and listed in Who's Who of American Women, as well as Who's Who of International Leaders. In addition to women's issues, Ms. Eastman speaks internationally regarding the importance of human respect as it relates to race, color, culture, age, and gender. She will be facilitating an international conference where speakers and participants from many nations will be able to discuss issues that are unique to women on a global basis.

Linda Ellis Eastman is also founder of The Professional Woman Speakers Bureau and The Professional Woman Coaching Institute. Ms. Eastman has dedicated her businesses to increasing the self-esteem and personal dignity of women and youth around the world.

Contact
The Professional Woman Network
P.O. Box 333
Prospect, KY 40059
(502) 566-9900
lindaeastman@prodigy.net
www.prowoman.net
www.protrain.net

INTRODUCTION

Linda Ellis Eastman

As a woman, you face challenges daily on an emotional, mental, and physical level. Oftentimes, you are left feeling as if you must face these obstacles alone. This book is written for you, the reader, to provide support and guidance through life's often difficult journey.

May the chapters of this book encourage you to face all obstacles head-on with courage and confidence. You are not alone in life. Remember that women on a global basis are presented with unbelievable challenges. We must support one another and constantly create ways to overcome the barriers which have been presented to us.

This book will contain chapters which, hopefully, will make your life less complicated. They are designed as a road map for life so that you are able to navigate with confidence and able to avoid many of the barriers that have been placed upon life's highway.

WOMEN'S SURVIVAL GUIDE

FOR OVERCOMING

OBSTACLES, TRANSITION & CHANGE

ABOUT THE AUTHOR

JENNIFER P. DAVIS

Jennifer is a human resource professional with more than thirty-five years of experience in corporate, manufacturing, public, and private sector organizations. She is President/CEO of *Jennifer P. Davis & Associates, LLC,* a minority owned business, which she started in 1997 following her retirement from IBM Charlotte.

During her tenure at IBM, Jennifer spent most of her career in executive management level positions managing annual budgets of up to forty-three million dollars. In addition to her management experience, Jennifer provided advice and counsel to the Site General Manager on personnel matters affecting a site of more than 3500 employees and 300 managers. She has written policy, continues to deliver leadership and management training, and develops programs designed to improve employee morale and increase organizational productivity. She was and is still sought out for her problem-solving ability and to provide direct and valuable guidance regarding sensitive issues involving harassment, discrimination, and unfair treatment in the workplace.

A much sought after motivational speaker, Mrs. Davis often entertains and inspires her audiences with songs, information, timely advice, and numerous anecdotes regarding her personal and professional experiences. A talented writer, Jennifer writes editorial columns for *The Gaston Gazette.* This is her first book publication.

Mrs. Davis was first elected to the *Gaston County Board of Education in 1996 and i*n December of 2002 was elected as the first African-American to chair that Board. She is a volunteer in many community organizations and has received numerous awards and honors. She also hosted a weekly radio show known as "Shammah Time" *"for women, about women, to uplift women where men are always welcome."*

Mrs. Davis holds certifications in the following:
• Five Factor Personality Assessments
• Diversity
• Women's Issues

Contact
Jennifer P. Davis & Associates
P.O. Box 6175
Gastonia, NC 28056
(704) 864-5211
www.jpdavisonline.com

ONE

"YOU WANT ME TO DO WHAT?" LESSONS OF LIFE

By Jennifer Davis

One month before my sixtieth birthday, I lost my mind....or so it seemed. I spent five days and four nights in the Pisgah National Forest in North Carolina with 27 other people that I barely knew. I went hiking (carrying a back pack that weighed approximately 50 pounds), climbed to the very top of Table Rock Mountain, repelled from a HUGE rock, completed a high ropes course (which concluded with a bungee jump that sent me flying approximately four stories in the air), slept _under_ a tarp...not a tent or a cabin...with three other people, and oh yes, spent one complete night in the woods in total silence. Alone! To some of you that may not sound so hard. In fact, there may be many of you who would welcome this experience. To you, I say, "Have at it." But, for me, consider this. I am not an outdoor girl. My idea of roughing it is stumbling in the driveway as I make my way from the car to the house. I have never lived alone. I have never been out of touch with my family for any extended period of time. I am petrified of snakes. I don't like bugs. And the thought of coming face to face with a creature (other than a dog or cat) with more than two legs is simply unimaginable. I like my easy chair, my book collection, and ice cubes delivered from the refrigerator door. I enjoy microwave popcorn, and I love to shop. I thank God every day for a hot shower, strong coffee, and a comfortable bed. I always have a plan A, and a plan B in case plan A needs to be adjusted. I had no desire to participate in this little adventure, and I was most concerned about breaking one of my carefully manicured nails. There was no hot shower. There was no shower, period. Coffee was instant and made with water boiled in a pot on a hot plate that we carried into the woods. There was no plan A, B, or C. The only plan I had was to get it done and go home. The trip itself was a small segment of a much larger plan. It was the team-building component of a year-long leadership institute whose overall curriculum was both attractive and intriguing. It was the curriculum that grabbed me, because I enjoy being a student. As participants, we were expected to clear our calendars as much as possible to accommodate the schedule, knowing that, at times, there might be conflicts. This portion of the curriculum, however, was not optional. Participation was mandatory and necessary, so that those of us who would spend the next year together could examine our leadership skills in an environment with few distractions, and bond as a team. In spite of the fact that I promised my undivided attention, and assured them I could bond quite effectively at the Marriott, I could not *"Plan B"* my way out of this if I wanted to participate in the rest of the institute. So, I decided not to grin, but to bear it. In the end, I found the experience to be the most uniquely rewarding challenge I had ever undertaken, and would not trade it for anything. I have no plans to do it again, but I wouldn't trade it, either.

So, what in the world would cause me to give up all the comforts of home, and step way out of my comfort zone to travel somewhere and do something I didn't **want to** do or **have** to do? I asked myself that very question right up to the time I boarded the van and headed deep into the forest. The answer came to me in the form of a gentle rebuke from one of my colleagues.

It came on the day that we were preparing to spend our last night in the woods. The last night was a test of skills learned during the trip. Each of us had to apply *individually* what we had learned and applied *together* over the past four days. That night, we had to create our own "home" in the woods, which included "pitching" your tarp in a bare space among the trees, finding stakes and tying secure knots so the tarp would not collapse, arranging your sleeping bag and other essentials, and then of all things, writing yourself a letter which would be mailed to you six months later. I had no intention of spending a night alone in the woods and recruited three others to participate in my rebellion. I emphatically stated to my colleagues that "I'm not doing that", when Dan turned and told me to drop the pretense. "Jennifer," he said, "we've got your number. You are not a quitter." It was as if I had been punched in the gut. He was right. Dan and the rest of the group not only "had my number", but discovered one of the very secrets of my soul. I am not a quitter. The night itself was by far the most frustrating and frightening time of my life. It was intended, among other things, to be a time of reflection, and for me, it achieved its purpose. It was not until much later that I grasped the full meaning of Dan's comment. The fact that he said "we've got your number" meant that not only were others watching me, but they were discussing me, as well. I did not waste my solitude.

I have recounted this adventure several times over the past months to anyone who would listen. I am still utterly amazed that I did this, and have difficulty describing some of my experiences or even looking at pictures. But, there is no doubt in my mind that I uncovered some "soul secrets" which are really lessons that have sustained me through the changes of life… its good times, bad times, and challenges.

The secrets of my soul, and yours, are really the lessons of life that navigate and guide us through successful daily living. Why are they soul secrets? Because they are the elements that comprise the very essence of who you are, and often you don't know you have them until you need them. They are the things that keep you from falling apart in times of crisis. They are the things that cause you to continue to put one foot in front of the other when all you really want to do is sit down. They are the things that keep you coming back again and again and again when you don't see or sense any progress. They are the things that cause you to smile and cause others to wonder what you are smiling about. They are the things that cause you to be amazed at your resilience, attitude, and confidence. They are those things that perfectly align your heart with your mind and your gut. They are the secrets that cause you to mentally pump your fist in the air and whisper to yourself, "You go, girl" when you know you have just given your all to some effort and absolutely nailed the results! They are the things that cause you to face adversity with courage, optimism and hope. They are the things that will not let you quit.

If asked, can you tell others what makes you tick? Do you know why you are the way you are, and can you perfectly articulate the answer to that question? You should know the answer, and it should be delivered with confidence, conviction, and certainty. Your response will serve as an inspiration to others and a source of encouragement for you.

Somebody is always watching you, and they may be discussing you, as well. Let your walk, talk, and persona be a witness for who and what you are. You don't have to spend five days in the woods (unless you want to) discovering those soul secrets. More than likely, you have spent most of your entire existence cultivating and practicing them. Being able to successfully overcome life's obstacles and challenges requires true self examination, time, attention, and a conscious understanding of what those secrets are. In other words, you have to know that you know what makes you tick. And, in case you have not affirmed those secrets, here are five steps to pilot you on this journey of self-discovery.

Discovering Your Soul Secrets

Step 1: Evaluate and enhance your personal relationship with God. No matter how close a relationship you may have with your family and friends, there will be occasions when you can't share with them, seek their advice, or ask for their help. It may not necessarily be a matter of trust. It may simply be that any attempt to share your thoughts and feelings seems inadequate at best. God intimately understands your deepest thoughts and emotions, and honors each and every one of them. You may attempt to share them in prayer, but in those times when you can't seem to find the words of prayer, the Spirit of God will pray for you. You cannot go plunging into the "forests of life" without a personal relationship with God. It can and will sustain you through anything. While in the real forest, I reminded God of His commitment to that covenant relationship and His promise to never leave me alone. It kept me through that long night in the woods, despite my fear and frustration.

Have you talked to God today?

Step 2: Spend time alone. Spending time alone doesn't mean you have to close and lock your doors, or put everybody out of the house. There are a number of ways and methods for you to accomplish this. Review the number of opportunities available to you each day to spend time with yourself. This may be in your car, your home, at the gym, in your office, a quiet lunch, and yes, even while shopping. It may be a time of solitude and reflection, or a time when you just embrace the environment around you. The important thing is to recognize that each of us needs time alone to elicit, evaluate, and examine who and what we are. It is a perfect time to cultivate your relationship with God. Talk to Him and let Him talk to you.

Think about your routine and list at least three places or times each day when you are on your own:

1. _____
2. _____
3. _____

Step 3: Be honest with yourself. You can fool anybody anytime you want by simply adjusting the truth. (Better known as telling a lie, or just plain faking it.) Relationships are built on trust and honesty. If you can't be perfectly honest with yourself and acknowledge your strengths as well as your weaknesses, then do not expect to be honest with anybody else. Relationships built on dishonesty are fraudulent, and have no value because they are not real. Personal integrity begins and ends with you. What God thinks of you matters far more than what others think. He knows the truth, the whole truth, and nothing but the truth, and loves you anyway. You can't fake Him out. When you are not authentic, others will detect it and credibility is lost. Loss of credibility erodes trust and trust is difficult to regain. Besides, what others ***think*** of you is far less important than what you ***know*** about yourself. Be brutally honest in your self-evaluation, affirming strengths and acknowledging areas that need to be improved.

Complete the following sentences with a statement that accurately describes you:
I am a person of purpose and value, and my strengths are: _____

_____

_____

I want to be the best person I can possibly be. I need to address :

_____

_____

Step 4: Identify Your Personal Values. I call this "the little man in my gut" syndrome. Think about it. We are living in a fast-paced, rapidly changing society. All of us have developed some degree of a "microwave mentality". We want everything done quickly, so we can move on to the next item on our list. Often you may find yourself engaging in tasks without really giving any thought to why you are doing them, or even what the anticipated outcome may be. Why do you do this? Because everything around you says, "Get it done, get it done, and get it done." Consequently, you may be so busy "getting it done" that you haven't given any thought to why you are doing it. This is foolish. To ensure a purposeful and rewarding life, identify those tasks that contribute to and promote the values of life most important to you. "The little man in your gut" will tell you when those things are out of sync with your activities. It may be a task that is necessary to be done, but ***you*** may not be the one that needs to do it. So, how do you eliminate those tasks that, over the long haul, hold very little meaning for you? You begin by knowing and living out the priorities of your life….your personal values.

1) Start by making a list of all those things that are important to you: love, peace, joy, happiness, faith, family, friends, success, safety, health, self-esteem, security, wealth, etc., remembering that *Step 3* says you must be brutally honest with yourself.

2) Study your list.

3) Write a sentence, if necessary, about each item on your list, what it means to you, and why.

4) Refine the list carefully. Relate one item to another, if that will help. Rationalize in a very practical and realistic manner why each item is on your list, and determine which ones really don't hold much meaning for you. Walk away from it for a while. Meditate on those values. Prioritize your list and eliminate those that don't seem important. Work at it until you have refined that list to those four items that "the little man in your gut" won't allow you to eliminate, refine, change or combine. These, in all likelihood, are the personal values that would totally change the person you are, and wish to be, if you were to abandon them.

5) Tuck them away in your heart, soul, and mind, and be prepared to share them when asked, "What makes you tick?"

The four most important personal values to me are:

1. _____

2. _____

3. _____

4. _____

Step 5: Take Care of Yourself. I have an older brother who, at the end of every conversation or visit, always says, *"Be good to yourself."* Many of us often say to another, "Well, take care of yourself" in a casual, carefree manner. I realized one day that this phrase, that we often take for granted, has the powerful potential and capacity to encourage and motivate others. I have often used it in speeches, classes, group sessions, and at graduations, providing my own interpretation of the statement's relevance to living a life of peace and contentment. Taking care of yourself means doing what is necessary for your physical, emotional, and spiritual well-being. It means engaging in those activities that help you promote a positive self-image, healthy outlook, and an attitude of hopefulness, rather than helplessness. In short, it's all about loving yourself. Every day the world will send you some kind of "you-can't, you're-not, you-won't, you're-not-good-enough" message. There will be a message, verbal or non-verbal, subtle or overt, that says you're too short, too tall, too old, too young, too fat, too skinny, the wrong color, the wrong race, not smart enough, too intelligent, too fast, too slow…. well, you get the picture. Your job is to love the person you are and the person you are becoming. Make a commitment to do something good for yourself and something good for somebody else every day. There will always be messages that imply something's wrong with you, whether true or not. You must deflect those comments with your own positive self-talk. Say good things to yourself and about yourself. Guard your heart and your spirit by filling your mind with good thoughts. Loving yourself will increase your self-esteem, deepen your confidence, and energize, and encourage you. Regularly treat yourself to a pedicure, manicure, or spa visit. Get your hair done. Buy a new shirt or piece of jewelry. Travel. Shop. Relax. Take a nap. Enjoy a bubble bath. Lose yourself in a good book. Watch your favorite television show. Call a friend. Sing. Skip. Laugh. Eat ice cream. Explore those things that make you feel good, and enjoy them to the fullest. Nobody should care more for you than you do for yourself.

List three things you do for yourself on a regular basis.

1. _____
2. _____
3. _____

Write three positive statements about who you are.

1. _____
2. _____
3. _____

Life lessons are sometimes very simple teachings that you have learned and practiced over time, guiding your thoughts and behaviors. They are produced from the secrets of your soul and, when allowed to be transparent, speak volumes about what you believe about yourself and others. Lessons such as:

- Develop your spiritual life. It will be the most important thing you do.

- Work hard. Be nice. Play fair.

- Fair and equal are not the same thing.

- **<u>Always</u>** do the right thing.

- Women need women. Women can immediately connect at the "soul" level.

- Mentor someone.

- Bite your tongue. You don't have to say everything you are thinking.

- Keep your promises.

- Guard your reputation. One day it may be all you have.

- Read.

- Be someone that others want to be around.

- Challenge yourself. Go to and through your fears.

- Be content and not complacent.

- Be real.

- Take care of others and they will take care of you.

Consider these very simple but profound lessons of life and never, ever quit.

This Chapter is dedicated to my family and friends who have allowed me to discover the secrets of my soul.

ABOUT THE AUTHOR

WILMA J. BROWN

Wilma J. Brown is President and Chief Executive Officer of Wilma J. Brown and Associates, a personal & professional development consulting and training organization dedicated to empowering lives both personally and professionally through seminars and workshops.

Ms. Brown is a certified professional trainer and consultant with over twenty years of experience in human resources, training and development. She's an expert in the areas of administration and management and holds a Masters degree in Occupational Technology, with emphasis in training and development, from the University of Houston. Prior to receiving her Master's Ms. Brown earned a Bachelors degree in Business Administration, with a concentration in marketing, from Texas Southern University in Houston. She is a certified trainer with The Professional Woman Network, specializing in diversity with an emphasis in women's issues.

Ms. Brown has conducted numerous training programs and workshops; she has worked in the public and private sectors for small and large organizations. Wilma J. Brown is known and respected as a consummate professional with a unique blend of knowledge and skills.

She is featured in the inspiring book by Olayinka Joseph, *I Would Save Mama First* (a celebration of motherhood) and *Women Reworked* (empowering women in employment transition) by Heather Resnick.

Ms. Brown is a native Texan. She is a member of the Professional Woman Network (PWN) –an international consulting organization specializing in personal and professional development, Toastmaster's International and the American Society for Training and Development.

She is available to keynote at workshops and seminars for organizations, churches, schools, colleges, businesses and corporations. Ms. Brown is available on a national and international basis.

Contact
Wilma J. Brown
P. O. Box 300514
Houston, TX 77230-0514
(281) 468-1130
wjbrown2@sbcglobal.net
www.protrain.net

TWO

EMBRACING CHANGE

By Wilma J. Brown

*"What is necessary to change a person is to
change his awareness of himself."*
— Abraham H. Maslow

We grow up. We go to school. We graduate. We get married. We have children. We divorce, and sometimes we have a repeat performance. We change in shape and size. Our hair gets thinner and changes to gray. Our interests change. Our thoughts change. The weather changes, technology changes. Change happens everywhere, all the time, and there is nothing you can do about it. It is a fact that the only thing constant in life is change!

The Myth of Change

If anything can go wrong, it will. Unexpected change is law. In order to embrace change, you have to expect it. Change happens. It is a constant in our world. Change is associated with negative circumstances and outcomes. Most people don't like change, because their comfort zone is going to be invaded and they automatically expect the worst. People set themselves up for failures. Changes sometimes can overwhelm. We should expect change, whether we want it or not. We may not like change, but it continues to be all around us. For most of us, change is uncomfortable and threatening. What most people don't realize is, change is part of life.

How Do You React to Change?
List three reactions when you are faced with a change.

1. _____

2. _____

3. _____

Let me share how I reacted to change when I lost my job three times during my career. It was something about this third time that made me decide that I would not go through this again. This last time prompted me to look at things in my life in a different way. I decided that this is it for me. This will not happen to me again. It was not just talk; I took **action**. It meant going back to school, looking at my life, and deciding what I wanted to do when I grew up. In order to do this, I had to make some serious changes. I asked myself the following questions. (You may want to consider these for yourself.)

1. What do I enjoy?

2. What have been my experiences?

3. Is it to my advantage to return to school?

4. How would I benefit from an advanced degree?

5. Can I do this?

6. What will be the time frame?

7. How badly do I want it?

These questions can be applied to other life situations, and you very well should have your very own questions.

Fear Factor

When I answered these questions, I was afraid to do something new. This would take me way out of my comfort zone. Deep down I knew I would have to change because, if I did not make a change in my life, I would continue to run up against a wall, the same wall.

Change can also be empowering. Change never comes without a challenge, or an invisible gift. Something good comes out of change most times, and we have to learn to embrace it as a part of life. You must change your thoughts and actions.

What are the top five reasons you are afraid of change?

1. _____

2. _____

3. _____

4. _____

5. _____

Embrace Change

Let me share how you can embrace change.

1. Accept Responsibility for Your Past.

Let go of any negatives from the past. It is the past, and you should let it go; you cannot move forward until you do this. Forgive yourself and others. My mentor says all the time, "If you continue to do the same thing, you continue to get the same results." When you get sick enough of your life, the direction in which it is moving, and not improving yourself, you **will** do something different for different results.

In the business world, the definition of insanity is doing what you have always done, and **expecting** different results. Let's not lose sight of the process to change. You have to embrace it.

2. Accept Responsibility for Your Actions.

Erase 'blame' out of your vocabulary. Blame is a negative energy, and removing it will leave room only for the positive. When you are positive, you will be better able to appreciate the good things you have, the good choices you make, and you'll be able to look forward to the future with enthusiasm, knowing that you are in charge of your future.

3. Develop a Positive Connection to Your Future.

It is not too late. The attitude that it is never too late is an example that whatever you decide to do, the important thing is 'to decide' and **do** something. There is no expiration date on taking action.

4. **Each New Day is a Learning Experience.**

Every day is a new beginning, so get into the habit of embracing each day with a positive mindset. You very well can determine what type of day you experience. Whatever happens, learn from it. *"The first step towards change is acceptance. Once you accept yourself, you open the door to change. That's all you have to do. Change is not something you do. It is something you allow."* —Will Garcia

5. **Look at Change as Building Blocks.**

Begin with one or two changes and build as you go along. Do not try and change too many things at once, for it can be overwhelming, and you are setting yourself up for failure. The more order you manage to maintain, the less confusion you will have to overcome, and you will not be forced into multi-tasking.

Change will only be embraced when you accept it as it comes. When change comes, it is a time to stop and look at where you are in your life and what it is you need to adjust to the change. Instead of focusing on what is wrong, think of all you have, what you have experienced, learned, and enjoyed in your life, and what you still want to accomplish. Taking the time to reflect on your life can help influence a proactive outlook, regardless of the situation.

6. **Allow Yourself Time to be Grateful.**

Always be in a state of gratitude. If we do this, it takes our mind off the negatives and what we don't have. If we practice gratitude, it can only be a positive perspective.

List three things for which you are grateful for right now.

1. _____

2. _____

3. _____

Steps to Change

Change is good. Adapting, adjusting, and making modifications to changing circumstances will yield new opportunities, new ideas, and new perspectives.

Make a list of five small changes you'd like to make. (These could be new habits developed, small accomplishments, things you want, or tasks that need to be done. i.e. "I will organize files in the computer once a week." Or, "I will monitor my thoughts and actions towards others every day.") Give yourself a deadline to accomplish these changes.

My list of 5 changes:

1. _____
2. _____
3. _____
4. _____
5. _____

What has happened in your life that has changed recently?
List three recent changes in your life.

1. _____
2. _____
3. _____

What will you do to accept these changes?

Change 1: _____

Change 2: _____

Change 3: _____

What Will You Do When Obstacles and Setbacks Occur, and How Will You Handle Them?

This is a major question to ask yourself when change occurs. The obstacles and setbacks will test your perseverance. Use obstacles as a means to test your resolve, and to find the positive in everything. Are you strong enough to face them? As you embrace change, add affirmations to help along the way. Positive self-talk affirmations are great incentives in helping yourself to handle changes we go through in life. Put them on paper or a 3" x 5" index card and carry them with you all the time. You are never bored if you have something to read to keep you motivated daily. Write your affirmations as if they were already true. Believe in yourself.

Some Examples of Positive Self-Talk Affirmations

- I am happy.

- I am deserving of more in life.

- I am a worthy person.

- I belong.

- My positive feelings create my reality.

- I will not give up.

- I am wise and loving.

- I embrace every day of this wonderful life.

Tailor your affirmations for yourself and what is happening in your life. Change them as you progress, and periodically look to see where you are. Monitor the progress and adjust as you face obstacles. You may include a meditation, a morning ritual to get the day off to a positive start, or have an evening routine to reflect on the day. In other words, all of these steps are part of a process. Be mindful of these changes, and reward yourself for your progress.

When repeating affirmations, say them with **feelings** and **believe** that you have already achieved them. They should be written in the present tense. **I can't say it enough – write your affirmations as if they were already true!** Remember, your actions are linked to what you put on paper.

"It's the repetition of affirmations that lead to belief. And once that belief becomes a deep conviction, things begin to happen."
— Claude M. Bristol

Overcoming Resistance to Change.
No matter how careful we prepare ourselves for change in life, or how well we execute being in control, there will be resistance. People fear uncertainty. The old way was fine, and there is no need to change mindset! Acknowledge your fear of change and let go. If you do this, you can stay in touch with why you resist change in the first place.

When things happen in our lives – make a concerted effort to "accept" them as they occur. Trust me, this is not easy, and yet it is something we must encounter and work on daily.

What Will You Do to Accept Change?

We must learn to embrace change, for it can be a new opportunity to grow, to heal, and face some real challenges. Keep in mind, unexpected change can be exhilarating and positive. The surest way to deal with any change is to focus on *solutions* and not the causes. And most of all, don't blame others. Take the time to think through changes as they occur. If you deal with life's changes as they come your way, on our own terms, you will be a stronger, better person for having looked change in the eye. Become a catalyst for change, and know that change is a healthy and powerful force. If you are not pleased with the direction your life is moving, you make the change!

I challenge you to take a serious look at your life, and decide that you will embrace change head-on – starting today.

ABOUT THE AUTHOR

RIKI F. LOVEJOY-BLAYLOCK

Riki F. Lovejoy-Blaylock, is a returning author in the PWN Series, having completed her works in *Becoming the Professional Woman* and *Overcoming The Super Woman Syndrome.* Her experiences as a business owner in the man-oriented construction industry affords her the ability to talk from the heart about successes and how setting goals are an important step to achieving successes. Entering the construction industry in 1985 as a receptionist, Riki knew she wanted to be at the top some day. Her main goal was to get her Bachelor's degree and after almost 24 years of taking night classes in between work travel and starting two separate businesses, she received her BS in Business Management with a minor in Management Information Systems at the age of 42! She also has a degree in Construction Technology. Her dream began at 17 years of age! Riki certainly understands the process of setting goals and sticking with them until the goal is met.

Riki has worked for major general contractors in the Orlando, Florida market as a Project Manager and owned a carpentry subcontracting company in the early 90's. Additionally, Riki has worked on construction projects in BeiJing, People's Republic of China and the Caribbean. Currently Riki is the Executive Director for *RFL Consulting Solutions, LLC*, a construction management consulting firm, with management contracts on projects throughout the country.

In addition to the BS degree, Riki is a certified Minority Business Enterprise through the Florida Minority Suppliers Development Council as well as a certified Woman's Business Enterprise through the National Women Business Owners Corporation. Riki is continuously named to the Cambridge Who's Who of Business and Professional Executives and most recently was elected as the Region 3 Director for the National Association of Women In Construction, another long-time goal finally met.

Contact
Riki F. Lovejoy
Executive Director
RFL Consulting Solutions, LLC
5607 Bay Side Drive
Orlando, FL 32819-4046
Office: 407.443.3423
Fax: 407.612.6300
Email: rlovejoy@rfl-consulting.com

THREE

SETTING GOALS FOR SUCCESS

By Riki Lovejoy-Blaylock

Man is a goal- seeking animal. His life only has meaning if he is reaching out and striving for his goals. — Aristotle

Success – we live our lives to be 'successful'. Every action, every decision, and hopefully all we say in our day-to-day life, become building blocks to our "successfulness". In all areas of our life, we want to be successful – as a wife, a lover, a mother, an employee, or maybe even as a business owner, but most importantly as a **woman**! But what is success – who provides the 'measurement' of what success is? According to the *New World Dictionary of American English, Third College Edition*, success is "a favorable or satisfactory outcome or result; the gaining of wealth, fame, rank, etc." Okay, so when will we reach the 'satisfactory outcome', or when will we acquire 'wealth, fame, or rank'? How do we get to this 'favorable result'? Does success _only_ mean 'wealth, fame, rank, etc.? What is *your* definition of 'Success'?

Success is a destination, and usually it's a very long drive to get there. Although you may want to arrive at Success some other way, you really won't be able to have someone else take you there; not by plane, train or bus – but for the most part you will need to drive yourself to that final destination. And just like any other unfamiliar destination, you will need a plan to follow – The Map. The Map that tells where the destination is, the roads you should take, and what the landmarks are along the way.

Again, what does Success look like? Where is it? What does the Map look like that will get you there? The honest answer is that only you can define or know what *your* Success looks like. Only you can know what *your* Map looks like. Hopefully, within these next few pages, I can quit with all the metaphors and help you understand a little better about defining or finding your Success and plotting your Map.

As a child you had moments when you daydreamed about what your life was going to be like tomorrow, your first day of elementary school, or the next year when you moved on to junior high and then the big one – What you were going to be when you grew up! Well guess what! Those daydreams were your first steps in setting goals. You started *envisioning* what your SUCCESS was going to look like when you were a young child realizing you really did have choices in life. Unfortunately, along the way, you probably had naysayers that "taught" you that lofty dreams are not realistic, not obtainable, and that goal setting was a waste of time, time that you just didn't have as you lived your day-to-day life. You gave up on setting any meaningful goals. So now you are reading this *Woman's Survival Guide for Overcoming Obstacles, Transition & Change*, which tells me that you are ready to change your thinking and become the ultimate person you know you are. You are ready to define your SUCCESS and plot your MAP... so here we grow...

Let's go through some steps for setting your goals.

1. ***Daydream*** – (*There are some people who live in a dream world, and there are some who face reality; and then there are those who turn one into the other.* —Douglas Everett) The subconscious mind is an incredible part of our being. Scientific studies have proven how the subconscious can and will define our actions, and ultimately define what we will become. The late Earl Nightingale, dubbed the "Creator of the Self-Improvement Industry", conducted a 20-year study on what made people successful. His end result – *we become what we think about.* So start daydreaming about what you want to be when you grow up. Start re-defining your Success by daydreaming what it is to be successful.

2. ***Understand Your Values and Take Yourself To Your Future.*** *(Never measure the height of a mountain until you have reached the top. Then you will see how low it was.* —Jacqueline Kennedy Onassis*)* – Goals have been more succinctly defined by the Time Thoughts organization as a "well-defined target that gives you clarity, direction, motivation and focus." Your goal setting is not just about professional growth; it is a self-improvement journey that also takes you to these "value landmarks" along the way – family and home, spiritual and ethical, social and cultural, financial and career (where we mostly think goals apply), physical and health, and your mental and educational needs. You should look at each of these aspects of your life and understand your value in them – what do you mean to them, what do they mean to you. Envision what your ultimate Success in each of these values looks like. As you begin to set your goals for these 'landmarks' and have a clear understanding of your values and what you believe your future is to look like, you

will find it easier to set your goals. More importantly, your road to Success will be a lot less bumpy, because you will not be fighting with the conflicts of your goals against your values. Ultimately, the two will be as one, and the road will be smooth sailing!

3. ***Write Your Goals*** – Okay, you have now done all this thinking, all this soul-searching, and you have a clear vision of what Success will look like for you. It's time to make your Map! Let me take this moment to be straightforward, honest, clear, and any other word that might make this point to you – your journey on this Map will not be a straight path. AND, for the most part, it's probably not going to be a short trip – nothing really worthwhile is a short trip. But it WILL be the best trip you will ever take, especially when you reach your destination – Success.

> *The difference between a goal and a dream is the written word.*
> — Gene Donohue, Founder of Top Achievement

So what do you actually write? Well, this will differ from person to person. Only you know what you need to keep yourself on track, focused on the goal. Do you need details, or are you the type that just needs the "summary" to get the whole picture? Whichever method works for you, I would suggest at minimum listing the "landmarks", i.e. family and home, physical and health, etc., what your value is to each (what it means to you, what you mean to it), and <u>what you envision as Success</u>. This last item is a must-write on your goals list. Not only is this what the goals list really all about, but writing this goal is for your subconscious mind. Your subconscious needs this "picture" to know what you will become.

And don't just write, for example, "I want to lose weight" (for your physical/health landmark). Provide as much detail for your subconscious mind so that it knows what you are to become (remember you *become what you think about*). Write a time frame. Let your subconscious know how much time you have to accomplish its mission, or by when you want to have it accomplished! And be reasonable. You can't lose 30 pounds in 30 days. So now you may have something written down that looks like "Physical and Health – I want to lose 30 pounds by 12/31/2007 so that my re-wedding dress (which I hope will be a Vera Wang) looks stunning!" Yes, my husband and I are renewing our vows (I call it the re-wedding) on 12/31/2007, our 10th Anniversary, and I want to look stunning – not for my husband, not for my guests and family – but for ME! After all, this is my Success, my goal. But doesn't the new goal description let you see what my Success looks like? If you, the reader, can now envision what my Success looks like, you can imagine what my subconscious is now doing and planning!

Now, this goal example was a simple one, and with a relatively short time frame. If you are going to set goals that will re-shape your life, you need to understand that you are setting goals with your future in mind, and this journey will not be a short trip. This is not to say that you still don't need the "short trips" along the way. Like our weight loss goal example, "short trips" are your reassurances. By knowing you can achieve goals, no matter how small, the more motivated you will be to continue working toward your higher goals. And setting higher goals is necessary. You need to push yourself out of your comfort zone, yet you should be careful not to over-do it. You want to set a balance of "lofty" goals and "realistic" goals. The main objective here is to get you to set the goals and write them down!

Actor Yul Brynner said it several times in the movie *The Ten Commandments*, – "So it is written, so it is done." Writing your goals will make it happen for you – I and all of the other self-help gurus can pretty much guarantee this for you. But writing your Map is not the end. Now you must use this Map you have plotted.

4. *Use Your Map* – *(You may encounter many defeats, but you must not be defeated. In fact, it may be necessary to encounter the defeats, so you can know who you are, what you can rise from, how you can still come out of it.* —Maya Angelou) – You have now written your very descriptive goals and created a tool that should become a part of your daily routine. You should review your Map daily, maybe even twice or more a day! Many goal setting handbooks suggest reviewing in the morning and again as you are going to bed. This process reaffirms your commitment to the goals.

You've done a lot of work to come up with this goals list and its timeframes, but how committed are you to the rest of the process? There will be prices to pay to achieve many of your goals. By routinely reviewing your Map, you are committing to your subconscious the vision of your life. You are continuously reminded of what it's going to take to achieve the goal, and then you reaffirm your commitment to the goals. You will also realize that sometimes the goals may need to be changed. And, not necessarily because the goal you set is not obtainable, but because you realize you can obtain even more. The journey to your Success should be a fun, educational, sometimes heart-wrenching, but always an awesome journey. Changes (also known as detours) can be expected; mistakes (oops, wrong turn) will be made, but you will always, if you continuously use your Map, find the right path again, and you will have learned something – hopefully something good, but possibly something bad – along the way.

5. ***Share Your Map*** – This can be tricky. Remember the "naysayer" that "taught" you that dreaming was a waste of time; especially when you are focused on living your day-to-day life? These are not the ones you want to share your dreams/goals/Map with because they will never understand it, and more importantly, will be incapable of encouraging you in the moments of doubt that you will have. Think about the influential people in your life and clearly understand who your consistent cheerleader is. For me, I am lucky to have two best girlfriends that say, "Go, Riki, Go, Riki" without the "but...". My husband and my brother, with whom I am very close, are more cautious cheerleaders who occasionally have a "but"; however, they are good for me, because they also keep me somewhat grounded. And unfortunately, I have others that I'm close to that have never been real cheerleaders, mostly because they don't know how. The Map is shared in its entirety with the girlfriends, partially with the hubby and brother, and not at all with the others. Remember, the journey to your Success destination, most specifically with the high goals, will be a long road with many pit stops, wrong turns, detours, and bumpy roads along the way. You will need to turn to your cheerleaders to get you back on track, from time to time. And, for goodness sake, do turn to them; don't think you are failing just because you have to reach out occasionally. Remember, those that you have shared with will be just as excited as you when you reach your destination, and they will want to have been a part of your Success.

*My philosophy of life is that if we make up our mind what we are going to make of our lives, then work hard toward that **goal**, we never lose - somehow we win out.* — Ronald Reagan

6. ***Don't Give Up!*** – (*It never occurs to me that there are things that I can't do.* —Whoopi Goldberg) Have I mentioned that the road to your Success will be a long one? There will be moments in time, in your drive to the goal, that you are going to say to yourself, "Why am I doing this? What purpose does this accomplish? Who cares if I accomplish this?" Then the final boom – "I don't need to waste my time anymore. After all, it's been so many years!" You may not see the light at the end of the tunnel, and this will discourage you to no end. And you know what, there may be a couple of your goals that maybe need to be re-evaluated or postponed, especially if you have too many "high" goals. But if they made it to your original goals list, they were dreams of what YOU wanted for YOU. Goal setting should become a lifelong process for you. When you reach one goal, you need to set another. So maybe, if one of your goals that was on your original list needs to be re-prioritized and postponed to a later time frame, then do so, but DO NOT eliminate it from your list. Do not give up on your goals.

Once you have set your goals and committed them to your subconscious, you will be amazed at what is going to happen in your world. Your mind will seem clearer, you will have a higher energy level, and you'll develop a passion for succeeding; you will see the path to your Success. You will be more in control of your life, and the world will manifest itself unto you. Sound corny? Let me tell you a story....

I am very involved with a trade association that has helped me tremendously throughout my career and, in fact, has brought people into my life that have had significant affects on decisions made, goals set, and general life fun. In the early 90's I had a list of five goals that I wanted to accomplish, and I was working very hard to accomplish them all. During this period of my life I was a very focused individual that sometimes got in the way of myself! More importantly though, I was definitely seeing some lights at the end of some of these tunnels!

One such goal was to 'one day become the Regional Director' for this volunteer trade association. The opportunity to run for this position came in the mid-90's when I ran against a lady from my very own Chapter. I had been approached by several members throughout the Region who thought I would be very good at doing this job and, in fact, would be much better than my opponent. Against my better judgment, I entered the race, a little late, but still in time to do a bit of campaigning and getting my name 'out there'. The big vote took place. I lost! I couldn't believe that I lost! The number of people that were behind me just gave me such a sense of power that I just knew I would be the shoo-in. What the heck went wrong?

I believe my number one goal setting rule – provide detail – was the first mistake. "One day" does not define it well enough for the subconscious. Secondly, my first instinct was to not run, but I ignored this gut feeling. But I believe most importantly, that the world had not manifested itself to me – in other words, it was not my time to be this Region's leader. I had a few more challenges (or today I now view them as opportunities) and experiences that I had to go through first to be in a better place to achieve this goal. In 2006, I was finally elected as the Florida Regional Director for a two-year term starting October 1, 2007. Ultimately, the timing of performing this job may not be the greatest because of my hectic schedule, but it is probably the best time. The world (and my subconscious) knew this better than I did. And the ironies do not stop here with the win of this election. My installation will be at the National Convention which is being held in my hometown (the last time it was here was in 1992!) and the date of the installation will be on my Grandmother's birthday, who I believe is my guardian angel. Too cool!

Please note that we are talking about a goal that was set over fifteen years ago! (Have I mentioned the road to Success is sometimes very long?!) I tried and failed and wanted to quit trying to achieve this goal, but it was a goal on my original list. And although I didn't commit to it everyday since I lost, my subconscious (that amazing and wonderful subconscious!) remembered, and every time I was at a chapter meeting, a function, a regional conference, or national convention over the next 10+ years, I was reminded about this goal. It seemed like someone from the Region was always asking me, "When will you run again?" I was so set against not trying again that I would even say, "You had your chance once before . . . you missed out!", basically blaming it on the wrong vote instead of it just not being the right time. Subconsciously, though, this was still a goal to be achieved.

So, don't procrastinate. You've been reading this wonderful *Woman's Survival Guide* because you (or your subconscious) are ready to make some changes in some aspect of your life that you don't like. So start setting your goals, write your Map, share with your cheerleaders, and begin the fun process of working towards achieving your goals. Remember, *you become what you think about.*

As one of your cheerleaders, I found this magnificent writing that I felt needed to be shared with you because I know you will find your destination, Success.

Success comes to those who are
Willing to sacrifice
Their immediate gratification
In order to achieve
Long-term satisfaction.
You know what success means
Because you have devoted yourself
To accomplishing the goals
You believe in.
You are someone who reaches out for dreams
And continues to strive towards
Finding new ones.

You are a success
And should feel so proud
Of the motivation that you possess.
Keep believing in yourself,
And find happiness
In all the days ahead.
— Laura Medley

ABOUT THE AUTHOR

KARLENE EWING PEDERSEN

Karlene (Ewing) Pedersen serves on the International Advisory Board for The Professional Woman Network, and is a member of the Professional Woman Speakers Bureau.

Ms. Pedersen's career in Human Resources includes having served as Director of Human Resources for several healthcare facilities, Corporate Human Resources Director, and as the Director of a Surgery Center. She has been involved in several start-up programs and hospital mergers.

In 1990, she started her own consulting business, KE Consulting, which has been primarily focused on healthcare facilities. Ms. Pedersen has traveled extensively over the past 30 years, and is sharing some of the knowledge that she has learned in making the process of traveling safer and less stressful. She is also co-author of *Becoming the Professional Woman* and a brand new book *You're On Stage, Image, Etiquette, Branding and Style* in which she writes about the art of interviewing.

Contact
KE Consulting
P.O. Box 22395
Bakersfield, CA 93290
559-731-1051
Kewing100@aol.com
www.protrain.net

FOUR

TRAVEL AND SAFETY TIPS

By Karlene Pedersen

During your lifetime, you will probably spend a considerable amount of time traveling either professionally or for pleasure. The content of this chapter is based upon knowledge that I have gleaned from over thirty years of traveling. Most of the information is from personal experience, with some important data gathered along the way.

This chapter will provide information that will be valuable to you, whether you travel alone or with a companion. I am sure that some of the information will not be new to you, but perhaps presented in a way so you will "not forget" and make your traveling more enjoyable and safer.

BE PREPARED. Your best travel weapon is to be prepared. This chapter will focus on:

• Travel Tips

- Safety

    a.   Your personal safety

    b.   Safeguarding your identity

- Staying in Hotels

- Transportation

    a.   Driving

    b.   Flying

    c.   Walking

- Packing

    a.   Planning your wardrobe

    b.   Packing to eliminate wrinkles

Selecting a Place to Stay

There are numerous sites on the Internet where you can make hotel reservations at a discounted rate. Be aware of the fact that normally it is more difficult (and sometimes impossible) to cancel or make a change in your reservation if you use these discounted agencies. Make sure you are aware of their policies before committing.

It is safer to stay in a hotel where you can enter your room from an inside corridor rather than directly from the street or parking lot into your room. WHY? If you pull into a parking space alone and there is a "potential" mugger lurking around, you are a *defenseless target*. You will probably sit in your car for a few minutes, gathering together your purse, papers, etc......all the time you are being watched. Then you go to the trunk of your car and get your suitcase(s) and start towards your room. Well, you can see how much time the intruder has to catch you off guard.

Making Your Hotel Stay Safer

When you arrive at your hotel, if you prefer to self-park, it is a good idea to pull up to the entrance and unload your car so you will not be going through the unsafe practice described in the preceding paragraph. Most hotels will allow you enough time to get registered before you have to move your vehicle. Do you think valet parking is a lot more expensive? Well, check because sometimes that is not the case. Valet parking is always safer for you.

- If your car has a "valet" key, remember to lock the trunk and give the valet key to the attendant, instead of your regular key(s).

What are some of the precautions you can do to make your stay safer after you have gone through the checking-in process and finally arrived in your room?

1. Make sure you do not open your door before you have *positively* identified the person standing on the other side.

2. If the person knocking says they are there to provide a service – housekeeping, security, plumbing, etc., you can always call the front desk to verify that someone has indeed been sent to your room.

3. When I leave my room, I always turn the television on and hang the "do not disturb" sign on the door.

4. Lock your valuables in your suitcase. Since you can no longer lock your luggage when you fly, it will be necessary for you to be sure and carry a lock with you for use in your room.

5. If you are uncomfortable for any reason, you can always ask for security to walk you to your room.

6. If your room has an outside patio, make sure that door is also secured, both while you are in the room and when you leave. It is a good idea to close the drapes leading to the patio when you leave the room.

7. While you are in your room, secure it by using the chain lock and turning the lock in the door.

When you check out of the hotel, **do not turn in your "credit card type"** room key. There is a big possibility that your personal identification information and credit card information is contained in the magnetic strip. I realize that this is a controversial issue; however, it is better to be safe than sorry. I was informed by a lawyer, and also a former hotel employee, that your personal information is indeed on the strip and remains there until it is swiped to make a new key. If you have noticed, when you hand in the key it is normally thrown in a drawer.... a drawer that is accessible to quite a number of different people. SO JUST TO BE ON THE SAFE SIDE....KEEP YOUR KEY.

Write down some of the things you learned from the above section that you want to put into practice.

_____

_____

_____

_____

Traveling By Car

The first and most important thing to do is to make sure your car is in good running condition. Have the car serviced, and be sure to check the following:

• Adequate tread on tires

• Proper air pressure

• Hoses

• Air conditioning and heating

• Water level

• Headlights and taillights working properly

Organize your directions, maps, etc., before beginning your trip, and have them on the passenger's seat so you can easily refer to them. Even if you are going on a short trip that you are very familiar with, always carry a state map, in case of detours directing you into areas that you are not sure of.

I find it very helpful to write on a card in **LARGE** letters and numbers, the highways I want to take. You can quickly glance at it and keep on track without having to stop to look at the map.

Unsure of where you are? Never pull over to the side of the road, especially at night, to read a road map. This signals that you are lost makes you an easy target for danger. Drive to a safe place to pull off the road.

Always carry a camera in your car so you can take pictures if you are involved in an accident. Disposable cameras are great to have in the car.

Some of the items to carry in your car when you start on a trip so you will *BE PREPARED:*

• Water

• Snacks

    a.   String cheese

    b.   Nuts

    c.   Fruit

• Blanket

• Jacket

• Flash light (I also carry a small flashlight in my purse at all times.)

• Flares

List below additional items that you personally should carry with you:

1. _____

2. _____

3. _____

4. _____

5. _____

Safety Tips For Entering Your Car

• Have your keys in your hand before exiting the building. Do not wait until you get to the car and have to dig through your purse looking for them.

• If you have a remote entry, wait until you are close to your car before pressing the opener. Normally your car lights blink and/or the horn sounds, which signals to a hovering thief as to which car you are headed.

• If you see someone suspicious, return to the building and request security walk you to your car.

• Lock your car immediately upon entering it, and do not roll down the window, even if someone approaches you requesting "help."

Traveling By Air

As with hotel reservations, you can book through the Internet and save money. Just be aware of their change policies. Personally, I prefer to book directly with the airlines, either by telephone or the Internet.

You can get cheaper rates on certain days of the week. So be sure and check that out. With the airline I normally use, the cheaper days are Tuesday and Thursday. The fewer restrictions you request (i.e., time of day, day of week, number of stops) the better rate you normally can secure. Although I always request a non-changeable rate, I have always been able to make a change, and there has been no charge if the request was made due to my health or a close family member's health.

- You can place a 24-hour hold on a reservation to give you time to coordinate with hotel reservations, etc.

- If you will need assistance getting around at the airport, make sure that you inform them of this when making your reservations. You can be escorted to the gate in a wheelchair, if needed.

- Check to see what the weight restrictions are for your checked bags, as well as the carry on restrictions, because they are not the same for all airports and airlines.

    a. You will be charged from $25 to $100 for each bag that is over the weight limit. You can buy an inexpensive device to check the weight of your bag.

    b. You will have to discard any carry-on item that is on the restricted list.

Day of Your Flight

1. Allow extra time to get to the airport. Arriving two hours early will give you time to get through security, find your gate, and then sit down and "relax."

    - Deep breathing is a great way to relax.

    - Bodine (over-the-counter) is great for motion sickness and doesn't make you sleepy.

- Green tea is helpful for the stomach.

2. If you are "germ conscious", you might be more comfortable taking a small blanket and pillow so you do not have to use the ones provided by the airlines.

3. Be courteous....don't "hog" the armrests, and don't push on the back of the seat in front of you with your feet.

Security Check

- You will have to remove your shoes and jacket, so wear shoes that are easily removed. i.e., no ties or buckles.

- Anything medal will set the alarm off, so try to eliminate wearing such things as belt buckles, jewelry, or accessories that are not genuine silver or gold.

After Boarding Plane, Flight is Being Cancelled

- Immediately use your cell phone and call your airline's customer service to arrange for an alternate flight for you. This will save you the hassle of standing in line, competing with angry passengers over available flights.

- You can also get the information and quickly get to the hotel the airlines will be paying for.

Very Important Safety Suggestions, Whether Traveling by Car or Airplane

- Make sure someone has your complete travel itinerary, including flight information, hotel, car travel route, and expected time of arrival at each place.

- Keep copies of your passport and driver's license in a separate place from the originals.

- Walk with your head held high, giving the appearance that you are alert and very much aware of your surroundings.

Packing – Pack Less, Save Your Back

The biggest mistake most people make is *overpacking*. It took me several years and many "backbreaking" trips to realize this. You can pack more efficiently if you will Plan and Coordinate.

I take out a pad and pencil and make a column for each day I will be away. Then I write in each column what I will probably be doing each day, assign type of clothing needed, and bingo! It is almost done.

If you will organize your clothing by coordinating items and colors, you will need fewer items.

- One black, dark grey, or navy skirt or slacks with one jacket or sweater plus three tops gives you three different outfits, and no one will notice that you have worn the same skirt or slacks.

- Organize your jewelry by color and put in small plastic bags. Grab a bag and it is all there....you don't waste time looking for that pair of yellow earrings...it's in the little plastic bag with just the right necklace or pendant.

- Don't forget a nice linen handkerchief. I guess that "dates" me, but it adds a nicer touch than pulling out a paper one. However, they do have some very pretty tissues printed with flowers, pretty high heel shoes, etc.

Tips for Packing

Pack your blouses and tops in 1-½ gallon size zip lock bags. The ones with the slide zipper works best.

- Make a fold near the middle of each shoulder and slide into the bag.

- Zip almost closed and then squeeze out all the air and zip closed.

- Garment will be almost wrinkle-free. If you prefer, you can use tissue paper in the fold.

- You can put at least two items in each bag.

- No messing up your clothes when you are digging to the bottom of your suitcase for an item.

A great testimony to the use of these plastic bags....just today I took a blouse out of one that had been in my suitcase for two weeks, and it was not wrinkled.

Another great packing tip is to roll your garments, which takes up less space and prevents wrinkles.

If you travel frequently, you might want to consider buying a second set of cosmetics and keeping a makeup bag always packed. Before I started doing this, I was always forgetting an item, a razor, floss, etc.

Essentials

• Needle, thread, and small safety pins

• Extra pair of hose in your purse

• A small flashlight in your purse

• Wig tape has adhesive on both sides and can be used to

   .....mend a hem.

   ....secure a bra strap from sliding.

   ....fix a gapping neckline.

   ...secure strap on heels of shoes.

Useful Tips

1. A soft baby toothbrush makes a great eyebrow comb.

2. Use small zip lock bags to organize makeup, or secure liquids from soiling clothing.

3. Small container of Fabreze to remove odors from clothing.

4. Wrinkle free spray for clothing.

5. Green tea, which neutralizes acid in your stomach, counteracting bad breath originating from the stomach when you are nervous.

    • After a few nights of drinking a cup of hot green herbal tea before going to bed, I noticed that I woke up with much fresher breath.

6. Always make a list of the items you have packed in your suitcase, in case your luggage is lost. Just make sure you don't keep this list in your suitcase.

Whether You Are Traveling or at Home, Protect Your Identity

- Instead of signing the back of your credit card, put "photo ID required".

- Never print your Social Security number on your checks.

- If you have a P.O. Box, use it instead of your home address on your checks, or use your work address.

- Keep a photocopy of all your credit cards, license(s) (front and back) so you can have them cancelled immediately in the event of a theft.

- When traveling, always carry a photocopy of your passport. Keep it in a separate place from your original passport.

- If your credit cards are stolen, in addition to calling the credit card companies, call the three national credit reporting organizations immediately to place a fraud alert on your name, and also the Social Security fraud line:

  (1) Equifax: 1-800-525-6285

  (2) Experian (formerly TRW): 1-888-397-3742

  (3) Trans Union: 1-800-680-7289

  (4) Social Security fraud line: 1-800-269-0271

I hope you have enjoyed this chapter, and that the information will help to make your next trip more relaxed and safer. If you have questions or would like to discuss any of the information in this chapter, you may contact me at the numbers listed in my bio at the beginning of the chapter.

Notes:

ABOUT THE AUTHOR

PHYLLIS S. QUINLAN, RNC, MS

Phyllis S. Quinlan resides in Flushing, New York. She has over 30 years experience in the healthcare industry with 25 years at a management level in acute care and long term care/ short-term rehabilitation settings. Phyllis is also a consulting Feng Shui Practitioner and has practiced this complimentary therapy since 1999. She is presently pursuing her Doctorate Degree in Healthcare Administration at the Kennedy-Western University.

Phyllis is the president of MFW Consultants To Professionals, a Consulting Firm serving the educational, personal coaching, and managerial needs of individuals and organizations. As a certified legal nurse consult, she also serves as an expert witness to many attorney-clients.

Phyllis is a contributing author for the following PWN publications: *Overcoming the Superwoman Syndrome, Your on Stage: Image, Etiquette, Branding, and Style* and *Woman's Journey to Wellness: Body, Mind and Spirit.* As member of the PWN International Speakers Bureau, she is available internationally to assist the individual client and/or organization with professional development needs.

Phyllis' most cherished role is that of godmother to five fabulous young women. She wants to dedicate this chapter to her paternal grandmother Anna McFadden, her maternal grandmother Ellen Farley, and her mother Madeline Walsh. She named her Firm *MFW Consultants To Professionals* to honor their strength and memory.

Contact
Phyllis Quinlan, RNC, MS, CEN CCRN, CLNC
MFW Consultants To Professionals, Inc
147-20 35th Avenue #2B
Flushing, New York 11354
718-661-4981
mfwconsultants@mindspring.com

FIVE

STARTING YOUR OWN BUSINESS: UNDERSTAND THE FUNDAMENTALS

By Phyllis S. Quinlan

Although no official definition of entrepreneurship exists, the one generally accepted is,

"Entrepreneurship is the process of creating or seizing an opportunity and pursuing it, regardless of the resources currently controlled." My consulting firm is my third attempt at being an entrepreneur. Owning my own business has been a goal of mine for over 25 years. I am enjoying a good deal of success, considering that I do not currently consult on a full time basis. The lessons I learned from my first two efforts served me well.

The first lesson I learned was to do something you love. However, there is a big difference between being in business and enjoying your hobby. I invested a lot of money starting up a hobby instead of a business. I did not take the venture seriously, therefore no one else did. A respected colleague later advised to be passionate about being in business, but never fall in love with your product. If the market for your product changes, you risk losing everything. Being passionate about being in business means that you monitor emerging markets, anticipate changes, and see the next big opportunity that might affect your business and plan accordingly. He was right.

The second lesson I learned was that doing your homework is vital. I found myself ill prepared to respond to the day-to-day demands of business ownership. I did not understand business structure options, pricing challenges, and accounting obligations to the degree necessary to be successful. Let me share a few of the fundamentals with you.

Business Fundamentals

1. Understand why you want to be an entrepreneur:

   - **Not wanting to answer to a boss.** You still must answer to yourself. It is important to embrace the fact that each new client is a new boss.

   - **The desire to have more free time.** It takes an enormous investment in time to get any venture off the ground. You will find yourself constantly exploring new methods and technologies in an effort to multi-tasking. If you are trying to start a business while you are keeping you day job, free time will be a faint memory.

- **Leaving the rat-race behind.** Your day will not only be consumed with meeting your current client's needs, it will be consumed with making the next big sale, securing the next contract, and tapping into new markets. Taking that mental health day off or leaving on that two week vacation can be challenging.

- **Increased flexibility.** The degree of flexibility is very dependent upon the business you start. If your clients live in a 9am to 5pm work week, you will need to live within that 9am to 5pm structure.

2. Study the current market and try to envision where the trends are heading:

- Is the retail industry hot?

- Is the service industry on the upswing?

- Is there a market for freelancing at what you currently do best?

- Do you have a creative, hot idea? Do your instincts tell you it will sell?

- Never forget that there is opportunity in chaos. Is there something around you that is broken and needs your special talents to fix it?

3. Develop a business plan:

- You business plan should be simple and clear. If you cannot explain it easily to someone, rethink the plan.

- There are plenty of publications and online tools to assist you on this project. Obtaining professional assistance in developing a sound business plan could pay off later, when you are looking for investment capital or a line of credit from your banker.

- Lay out your basic business plan before making any initial investments. You will risk using precious start up capital in all the wrong places with having little to show for that investment. Include a timeline in your initial plan so you can monitor your progress and stay on track.

- In the beginning, pay yourself enough to live on. You can subsidize your salary with bonuses as the business grows. Part of your plan may be to pay down current debt over the next 12 months, so that you are in a better position to manage your day-to-day expenses on the salary you will pay yourself.

4. Decide on a storefront model:

- Do you need to rent an actual business or office space? Remember the three most important concepts for basing your business in the community: LOCATION, LOCATION, LOCATION. Don't be afraid to locate yourself down the block from your competition. Your strategy here is to cash in on the demographic research done your competitor, and foot traffic your competitor's advertising budget brings. Accepting your competitor's coupons has worked for many. Clearly, this strategy is only successful when your product and services are the very best.

- Will a virtual office space serve your needs? Having a wonderful business address in a prestigious downtown building can lend a perception of experience to a start up business.

- Can you be a home-based business? There are many advantages to this model.

  o Short commute.

  o Ideal for the stay-at-home mom.

  o Tax incentives (review with your tax accountant).

- Is a website all you need to get started?

  o Is it engaging?

  o Is it easy to navigate?

5. Gain a sense of pricing for your product or service:

   - Understanding the price the market will bear is vital. Too low and you do not make enough profit to stay in business. Too high and you cannot compete with your competitors.

   - As a consultant, my product is myself. I initially priced my services in the mid-range. I invested a good deal of sweat-equity until my reputation grew and my client base expanded.

6. Are you prepared to stay in business until you succeed?

   - Most new businesses do not survive past the first year.

- Each hard lesson learned should not be viewed as a failure, but rather as one step closer to your goal.

Generating Business

1. Develop a portfolio to demonstrate the scope of your skills.

    - Development of the portfolio can be time consuming and a potentially costly investment. First impressions are vital.

    - Be consistent in color, design, and font so you can establish your brand identity

    - Samples of your work are your best calling card.

    - Letters from satisfied clients are a good idea.

    - The portfolio can be mailed and/or presented at meetings.

2. Tell colleagues, friends, family, and neighbors about your new venture

    - Referrals initially can generate a large portion of your business.

    - Be ready to talk about your business/service spontaneously.

        o You will need to work on a three to four sentence infomercial that will have an high impact and generate questions and potential work.

3. Promote your business:

    - Attending meetings and networking can lead to referrals and work.

- Volunteer to speak at a meeting or facilitate a project. Let your colleagues see what you can do.

- Volunteer your services in the in the community/church/etc.

This has been a particularly successful approach for me. I have received several lucrative consulting and teaching contracts from referrals received from colleagues who have heard me speak on topics at meetings.

4. Conduct Cold Calls Using the Internet

- Mailed brochures often never make it past the administrative assistants. Emailing is the only true "mailing" that makes it past the gatekeepers.

- Surf the Net for potential clients. Many have their email addresses on their business websites.

- Compose a cover letter for the text of your email.

- Create a formal signature, consistent with your established logo/brand to sign off your cover letter. Here's an example:

MFW Consultants To Professionals, Inc
Phyllis Quinlan, RNC, MS, CLNC
mfwconsultants@mindspring.com
147-20 35th Avenue #2B
Flushing, New York 11354
718 661 4981

- Attach important items such as resume, fee structure, and samples to the email.

- Keep track of the sent emails for follow-up purposes.

This approach created my biggest breakthrough. Last year I emailed 108 attorneys and grew my certified legal nurse consulting business by 400% within 30 days.

Understanding Business Structures

1. Sole Proprietorship

The sole proprietorship is thought of as the quickest and easiest way to set up a business operation. You may already be operating a sole proprietorship. Little more than buying and selling goods or services is required. There are no prerequisites or specific costs in starting up this type of business structure. No formal legal filing is required. A sole proprietor need only register her name and secure any local licenses. It begins the minute you turn the key on your enterprise. You are the sole owner. The sole proprietorship is not a legal entity. The owner of a sole proprietorship typically signs contracts in her own name.

Because a sole proprietorship is indistinguishable from its owner, the sole proprietorship taxation is straightforward. The income earned by a sole proprietorship is income earned by its owner. Profits and losses are first recorded on a tax form called a Schedule C, which is filed along with your 1040. Then the "bottom-line amount" from Schedule C is transferred to the owner's personal tax return. This aspect is attractive because business losses you suffer may offset income earned from other sources.

A sole proprietor must also file a Schedule SE with Form 1040. A Schedule SE is used to calculate how much self-employment tax is owed. The owner does not pay unemployment tax on herself, although she must pay unemployment tax on any employees.

Advantages

- Owners can establish a sole proprietorship easily and inexpensively.

- Owners may freely mix business or personal assets.

Disadvantages

- Owners are subject to unlimited personal liability for the debts, losses and liabilities of the business.

- Business-related accident and the resulting legal actions can be brought against the owner and against all her personal assets.

- Owners cannot raise capital by selling an interest in the business.

- Sole proprietorships usually do not survive the death of their owner.

2. The General Partnership

Starting a general partnership is also a simple process. There are no costs or legal formalities. However, your attorney should advise you to have a detailed partnership agreement. Details in a partnership agreement should at least include:

- The amount of capital each partner is expected to contribute up front

- The rights and duties of each partners

- The agreed upon process for sharing profits and losses

- The required authorization for cash withdrawals and capital expenses

- The procedure for resolving disputes, or taking in new partners

• The procedure for dissolving the partnership

3. Incorporating

Anyone who owns a business may incorporate. Owner(s) of a business of any size can benefit from incorporating. Before deciding which type of corporation best suits your business needs, I strongly recommend that you consult with your legal or financial advisors.

The law views a corporation as a *fictional person,* or a *legal person* as opposed to a natural person. As a legal entity, the corporation enjoys many of the rights and obligations of individual persons. Five rights always exist for a corporation:

• The ability to sue and be sued

   ○ This gives the corporation access to the courts.

• The right to a common treasury

   ○ This gives the right to hold assets separate from the assets of its members.

• The right to hire agents

   ○ This gives the corporation the right to hire employees.

• The right to a common seal

   ○ This gives the corporation the right to sign contracts.

• The right to make by-laws

   ○ This gives the corporation the right to govern its internal affairs.

Types of Corporations

1. General Corporation (aka "C" Corporation)

A general corporation is the most common corporate structure. A general corporation can have an unlimited number of stockholders. It is usually chosen by those companies planning to have more than 30 stockholders or large public stock offerings. Since a corporation is a separate legal entity, a stockholder's personal liability is usually limited to the amount of investment in the corporation.

Advantages
- Personal assets are protected from business debt and liability.

- Corporations have unlimited life beyond the death of the owner.

- Tax free benefits such as insurance, travel, and retirement plan deductions

- Transfer of ownership facilitated by sale of stock

- Change of ownership need not affect management.

- Able to raise working capital through sale of stocks and bonds

Disadvantages
- More expensive to form than proprietorship or partnerships

- More legal formality

- More state and federal rules and regulations

2. Close Corporation

A close corporation is most appropriate for the individual starting a company alone or with a small number of people. There are a few significant differences between a general corporation and a close corporation. A close corporation limits stockholders to a maximum of 30. Not all states recognize close corporations.

3. Subchapter S Corporation

A Subchapter S Corporation is a general corporation that has elected a special tax status with the IRS after the corporation has been formed. Subchapter S corporations are most appropriate for small business owners and entrepreneurs who prefer to be taxed as if they were still sole proprietors or general partners.

S Corporations avoid double taxation because all income or loss is reported only once on the personal tax returns of the stockholders. For many small businesses, the S Corporation offers the best of both worlds by combining the tax advantages of a sole proprietorship or general partnership with the limited liability and enduring life of a corporate "C" structure.

4. Limited Liability Company (LLC)

The LLC is not a corporation, but it offers many of the same advantages. Many small business owners and entrepreneurs prefer the LLC because they combine the limited liability protection of a corporation with the "pass through"" taxation of a sole proprietorship or general partnership.

Advantages
- Protection of personal assets from business debt

- Profits/losses pass through to personal income tax returns of the owner

- Great flexibility in management and organization of the business

- LLC's do not have the ownership restrictions of S Corporations, making them ideal business structures for foreign investors.

- LLC's are now available in all 50 states and Washington, D.C.

Disadvantages
- LLC's often have a limited life (not to exceed 30 years in many states).

- Some states require at least 2 members to form an LLC.

- LLC's are not corporations. They do not have stock or the benefits of stock ownership and sales.

Another Option
If your are feeling a bit conflicted or in a time of your life when undertaking the full responsibility of business ownership is not a realistic possibility, there is yet another option for expressing your entrepreneurial self. Become an Independent Contractor and affiliate with other established entrepreneurs. Many entrepreneurs are not interested in taking on the burden and the responsibility of employees. Instead, they utilize the services of an Independent Contractor to service their client's needs and add to the depth of services that their particular business offers.

An independent contractor is a natural person, business or corporation, which provides <u>goods</u> or <u>services</u> to another entity under terms specified in a <u>contract</u>. Independent contractors are consultants, freelances, or free agents. Independent contractors often work through a <u>company</u> that they themselves own. Regardless, all are self-employed.

Disadvantages

- Independent contractors "withhold" their own federal, state and local taxes, unlike employees.

- Unlike an <u>employee</u>, an independent contractor does not work regularly for an employer, but works as and when required.

- Independent contractors are usually among the first to get the axe when slowdowns and layoffs occur.

- Contract jobs might be fewer, and you might find yourself competing more, bidding lower, and going without work for a while.

So what do you think? Do you have the right stuff? The information I have outlined above can serve as a checklist as you start your new venture. Keep in mind that regulations and laws are constantly under state and federal revision so be sure to consult your legal and financial advisors.

Entrepreneurship is not for the faint of heart. It is not a game or a hobby. It is the real deal. It will constantly challenge you, and force you to grow in ways you never imagined. It can be the best ride of a lifetime. If you decide to go for it, don't lose my name. I love networking with smart, brave souls.

References

http://www.stanford.edu/class/e145/materials/Characteristics.html

http://en.wikipedia.org/wiki/Independent_contractor

http://emerging-entrepreneurs.com/

http://wntrepreneurs.about.com/cs/makingthechoice/a/intrapreneur.htm

http://www.entrepreneurs.com

http://www.kiplinger.com/columns/starting/archive/2006/st0504.htm

http://www.motivatedentrepreneur.com/

http://www.teenanalyst.com/business/

http://en.wikipedia.org/wiki/Corporation

ABOUT THE AUTHOR

KERRY J DEGNAN

Kerry J Degnan is a professional speaker, trainer, and executive presentation consultant. Her professional background includes designing and developing both soft skills and technical training programs. Kerry has worked within both corporate and university settings, including the Center for Training and Development at Harvard University. Her background also includes designing and facilitating virtual classroom learning as well developing self-paced eLearning programs.

Kerry holds an MA in Organizational Communication as well as an MAE in Human Resources/Training and Development. She is currently pursuing a Master of Liberal Arts in Educational Technologies at Harvard University. She has also been an adjunct faculty member at several colleges and universities and has led communications skills and personal development workshops for many community-based organizations. She is also a Life Coach and Reiki practitioner who focuses on wellness and positive living for women in mid-life.

She is a co-author of the book *Self-Esteem and Empowerment for Women*.

Contact
Kerry Degnan
PMB 634
1770 Massachusetts Avenue
Cambridge, MA 02139
617-877-1075
degnanboston@aol.com
http://www.protrain.net/degnan.htm

SIX

RECLAIMING YOU

By Kerry Degnan

I'm sure many of us have days when we barely recognize the face staring back in the mirror. What happened to that young, inspired woman with her life ahead of her? That's exactly it: LIFE happened! Time zips by faster than a speeding bullet. Changes and life transitions occurred, whether we were conscious of it or not. It's easy to get caught up in day-to-day life and suddenly notice that everything changed while you were either sleeping or looking the other way. Mirror, mirror, mirror on the wall…where did time go? Where did that young woman go?

It happens every time I walk down a city street and notice that the admiring glances are for the younger women walking ahead or behind me. It also occurs when realizing that the newly hired co-worker is at least ten years younger, and possibly higher salaried. It happened to me in a graduate class when the Professor referred to me as the older generation. But what are those experiences all about? It could be an opportunity to smile and be thankful for being a beautiful light at your current age, someone who can mentor a younger co-worker, or an inquisitive student setting the example that lifelong learning is important at every age. Your own sense of empowerment is key to managing change, as well as interpreting life experiences.

Mid-life can bring a longing to reclaim one's true essence, and find meaning and purpose in various dimensions of life. If you've hit the mid-peak blues and feel like you're in a rut of one kind or another, it's time to face it head on.

Face It: Change and Transition are a Way of Life.

It's often during life's milestones or transitions that the winds of change are most evident. It can be as traumatic as a divorce, children leaving the nest, job loss or career transition, relocation, or the passing of a loved one. It's also very natural to move through the stages of change at your own pace. As mid-lifers, it can also be as eye opening as being called ma'am on a regular basis, forgetting things, or realizing that the flabby upper arms you see in the shower each day are really yours. It's easy to resist the changes that are occurring. The sooner you embrace those healthy, beautiful arms, or that milestone birthday that's looming ahead--the better.

It's all about YOU: What change or transition do you need to face head-on?

_____

_____

_____

Face It: There's No Going Back, Only Forward.

A new point in life can be an opportunity for tremendous personal growth. The key is not letting fear of change or perceived obstacles get you off track and stuck in the past or present. There's no going back to prom night, freshman year in college, first apartments, or other fantasies that make one reminisce about the good old days. If your first apartment was a tiny studio like mine with no air conditioning, why would you even want to go back? It's easy to focus on the sense of loss that is often inherent with transition, rather than on how change will make your life better now and in the future. Moving forward is not so much a choice, but a reality. Why not shape your own reality?

It's all about YOU: What changes will you commit to making over the next 30 days to move your life forward?

_____

_____

_____

_____

Face It: We're Constantly Changing, Whether We Realize It or Not.

"Time may change me, but I can't trace time" is a lyric from a popular 1970's song. When reflecting upon one's life experiences, it isn't always easy to pinpoint or trace change. Does it really matter? Isn't it exciting to be in a constant state of change? That powerful mind-shift can enable you to create your own positive change. Be proud of what you've accomplished, but treasure the experiences and opportunities you are having at your current stage of life. Be open to all of the wonderful experiences that lie ahead. Our experiences, whether good or bad, enrich our lives. Better that we mold and remold ourselves over time than be stuck in a mold we've outgrown physically, mentally, or emotionally. Don't let perceived obstacles keep you stuck in an old mold.

It's all about YOU: What perceived obstacle do you need to face in order to create positive change?

_____

_____

_____

_____

Face It: It May Be Time for a Tune-Up, Not a Tune-Out.

Just like the reliable car that occasionally needs a tune up, we take ourselves for granted, and don't always make time for tender loving care, or even basic maintenance. It may be a health goal, such as dropping a few pounds or making more time for you. At mid-life, there's an opportunity to recharge those batteries and get it in gear. Getting it in gear may be a new career opportunity, taking charge of your finances, traveling, going back for that degree, getting in shape, spending more time with your partner, finding a new hobby or interest, making new friends, or whatever you've been putting off or letting slide.

It's all about YOU: What aspects of your life need a tune up?

_____

_____

_____

_____

Face It: There are Interesting, Attractive, and Intelligent Women of All Ages Doing Great Things in This World. You Are One of Them!

Let's move from mid-lifers to mid-dreamers. If you think you're too old, or don't have the time, energy, or support needed to pursue your goals and dreams, consider these facts:

Women and Career: Many more women are starting their own businesses and stepping out of their comfort zones into unchartered waters. Do you have a dream of owning your own business or embracing a different career? Check out SCORE or your local business development center for information on free resources and workshops. Attend a Business and Professional Woman's club meeting, or contact an organization, such as PWN, to start networking. The web is also a good resource for researching a career change.

Women and Travel: According to the Gutsy Traveler, the average adventure traveler is a 47-year-old female who wears a size 12 dress. Where have you always wanted to go in the world? There are many travel and adventure clubs for women where you can travel alone safely and meet liked minded travelers in the process. It's never too late to see the world. If you are interested in volunteering, why not try a volunteer vacation? Organizations like Global Volunteers offer a variety of destinations and work projects. Why not do good while having a brand new experience at the same time?

Women and Money: Although women typically make less money than men, there's evidence they're actually better investors. According to a recent study by the National Association of Investment Clubs, women's investment clubs out-performed their male counterparts by a wide margin in nine out of twelve years. Where do you need to be in order to retire and live comfortably? Check out investment clubs in your area if don't already have a financial planner. Many adult schools offer workshops on "Women and Investing" that will also give you the opportunity to learn how to take control of your finances and make wise investments.

Women and Education: According to the American Association of University Women, sixty percent of nontraditional online learners are over 25 years of age and female. Distance learning is offering new opportunities and flexibility for women of all ages to return to school. What is stopping you from returning for that degree, or taking continuing education classes to enrich yourself? Many women's organizations provide scholarships or grants for women returning to school.

Women and the Boomer Generation: According to a 2005 U.S. Census Bureau statistic, 50.8% of the 78.2 million baby boomers are women. You are in good company! If forty or even fifty are the new thirty, you've got plenty of exciting changes, challenges, and opportunities ahead of you. What mid-dreaming goals will you set? During my 45th year, I made a list of all of the "cool" things I did during the first 1/2 half of my life. The list ranged from going in the funhouse alone at 5 years old, traveling to over 15 countries, enrolling in graduate school in my 40's, attending a St. Patrick's Day parade in Dublin, Ireland, and attending an amazing Tina Turner concert.

EMBRACE It: You are Pretty Cool Yourself.

Make your own list. What have you achieved? Are you a great parent? Taken a class you loved? Been a loving spouse? Built your dream house? Nurtured good friends? Switched careers? Great cook? Accomplished a personal goal? Traveled to that dream destination? Learned a new language? These amazing accomplishments have nothing to do with your age or dress size. Begin to reclaim those things that you love. To get started, think of at least 10 "cool things" you've done either this year, the last five years, or as I did—by a milestone:

1. _____

2. _____

3. _____

4. _____

5. _____

6. _____

7. _____

8. _____

9. _____

10. _____

EMBRACE It: You Have Plenty of Life Left to LIVE, and Plenty More to GIVE.

There are both big and small transitions in life. Celebrations such as bat mitzvah, Holy Communion, first date, prom, sending children off to college, being a mother—all of these are moments where we pass the torch to our daughters, nieces, and other young women the same way our mothers and grandmothers did for us. What about the dropped threads of your own life? Who were your mother, grandmother, and great grandmother? Weren't they once in your place in life? What gifts did they pass on to you?

What gifts will you pass on?

_____

_____

_____

_____

EMBRACE It: You've Got Power.

Make your own mid-dreaming list. Think of at least 10 more "cool things" that inspire you: Finish that degree? Visit Paris? Switch jobs? Start dating again? Form a Women's Circle? Find more meaning? Make new friends? Try yoga? Join a book club? Spend more time with kids or grandkids? Start a business? Take a wine tasting class? Sign up for a Latin dance class?

Get inspired! List at least ten more "cool things" to add to your mid-dreaming:

1. _____

2. _____

3. _____

4. _____

5. _____

6. _____

7. _____

8. _____

9. _____

10. _____

Your lists will surprise and amaze you. Chances are, your mid-dreaming list will grow way beyond 10 things. It's all about inspiration and finding true passion for life. My wish for you is to move from invisible to brightly visible. It means different things to each of us, but the core message is the same: the person you need to be most present and visible to is **YOU**.

Three steps to begin the process of reclaiming YOU:

> ***Get Clarity.***
> ***Trust your Intuition.***
> ***Find your Passion.***

It's as simple as that. Spirit, life, and love reside in all of us, whether we are the woman with the years of life experience, at a mid-life transition, or the younger woman in her own place in life. It is time to start reclaiming YOU. We're not mid-lifers, but truly mid-dreamers who are ready to reclaim our lives, spirit, and selves.

Watch out world!

Recommended Reading

The Gift of Change by Marianne Williamson

Excuse Me, Your Life is Waiting by Lynn Grabhorn

The Five Principles of Ageless Living by Dayle Haddon

Refuse to Choose by Barbara Sher

ABOUT THE AUTHOR

MICKI K. JORDAN, MLDR

Micki Kremenak Jordan is a mentor, trainer and coach. She has held a variety of management positions over the past twenty-five years. She has participated on Visioning and Strategic Planning Teams and is currently a member of the Leadership Development Team for Providence Presbyterian Church.

Ms. Jordan has a Bachelor of Science Degree in Sociology from the University of Iowa. After several years in the corporate world she obtained her Masters of Arts in Leadership in 2001 from Bellevue University. Ms. Jordan is certified in Diversity Training, Public Speaking and Professional Coaching. She holds the Certified Insurance Councilor Designation and is a member of the Professional Woman Network (PWN) and the National Association of Female Executives (NAFE).

Her passion is assisting others to recognize their true potential. Her plans for the future include developing and presenting small group seminars for college students and upwardly mobile career women. She also plans on doing more writing.

Contact
Micki K. Jordan
11066 Rodeo Circle
Parker, CO 80138
(720) 851-6964
mickijordan@yahoo.com

SEVEN

LIVING YOUR VALUES

By Micki K. Jordan

Define your life in your own terms, and live every minute consistent with the very best person you can possibly be. —Brian Tracy

Today is Mother's Day, May 13, 2007, and I have just spent the day with my eighty-nine year **young** mother. We began the day attending her church, The Church in the Wildwood, in tiny Green Mountain Falls, Colorado. The sermon was entitled, "It is About You." As Pastor Dave spoke, I became more aware that he was speaking of Living Your Values. His message dealt with responding to situations by who *you* are, not who *they* are. Isn't your response to a situation created by your value system? A value system developed from your environment, from the actions and beliefs of your parents, your teachers, your friends and your peers?

Values – what are they? Where do they come from? Why are they important? Values define who you are, what you stand for, and what you believe in. They are a reaction to a particular situation, possibly a stressful one. Values are things we consider to be special. An individual's behavior is defined by their values. They are positive qualities in our lives. Values are active, and they are motivators. The reasons why we do things are based in our values. Values will remain constant over time, and they are about what is right. They cannot be forced upon us by others. In order to be a value, it must be freely chosen. It takes thoughtful consideration to make a choice of values.

Where do values come from? All cultures have value systems. When our country was formed, the founding Fathers wrote the Declaration of Independence, expressing what they felt were important core values. Among these were Life, Liberty, Pursuit of Happiness, and Truth. Values are important, as they define who we are and what we stand for in life. They will show up in many things we do. They come from what we see, what we hear, and what we read.

They are not a one-time happening, but an integral part of our being. The values you choose to live by make it clear who you are and what you believe. If we live in accordance with our highest values, it will increase our self-confidence. Values are things we do; we live them. They are reflected in the choices we make and the actions we take. If our demonstrated behavior seems to be at odds with the values we feel we want to live by, it may be time for some life changes. Values are visible.

"Your attitude is an expression of your values, beliefs, and expectations."
—Brian Tracy

Types of Values

Values can be placed into several categories. They are often classified in four areas.

- **Personal Values** - Define you as an individual; they determine how you relate to people.

- **Cultural Values** – Connect you with a practice of faith and customs; they connect you with others of similar backgrounds.

- **Social Values** – How you relate to others in social situations. These involve family, friends, and co-workers.

- **Work Values** – Define the way you work and how you relate to your bosses, your co-workers, and to your customers or clients. They are your professional behavior.

Other classifications of values include:

- **Moral Values** – These are the values that society considers desirable; they are judgments of actions.

- **Core Values** – Also known as governing values. These are the cornerstones of everything you do and accomplish.

- **Living Values** – These are similar to core values. These are the personal values you want to achieve in your life.

Know thyself. —Socrates

Identifying Your Values

In order to develop a clearer picture of what is important as you live your life, let us begin with a list of values. Use this list as a guide. Many will not apply to you, and if there are others, please add them to your list. As you review the following values, think of situations and how you have reacted to them. Consider these questions:

- Which values do you truly embrace?

  1. _____

  2. _____

  3. _____

- What do you passionately believe in?

  1. _____

  2. _____

  3. _____

- What do you stand for?

  1. _____

  2. _____

  3. _____

Exercise

From the following list, circle 10 – 15 words that you feel are values that influence your actions and behaviors. (Or you may choose to build your own list.) Be careful to select values that are important to you, and not just ones you think you should have. Another way to think of it is, if you were given a year to live, what are the most important things to you and how you would live your life?) Suggested Values:

ACCEPTANCE	ACCESSABILITY	ACHIEVEMENT
ACTIVENESS	ADAPTABILITY	ADVENTURE
AFFECTION	AGGRESSIVENESS	APPROACHABILITY
ASSERTIVENESS	AWARENESS	BALANCE
BELONGING	BOLDNESS	BRAVERY
CALMNESS	CANDOR	CARE
CAREFULNESS	CHEERFULNESS	CLEANLINESS
CLEVERNESS	COMMITMENT	COMPASSION
CONFIDENCE	CONTROL	COOPERATION
COURAGE	COURTESEY	CREATIVITY
CREDIBILITY	CURIOSITY	DECISIVENESS
DEPENDABILITY	DETERMINATION	DIGNITY
DISCIPLINE	DIVERSITY	DRIVE
DUTY	EAGERNESS	EFFECTIVENESS
ENCOURAGEMENT	ENERGY	ENJOYMENT
ENTHUISIASM	EXCELLENCE	EXCITEMENT
FAIRNESS	FAITH	FAMILY
FEARLESSNESS	FITNESS	FLEXIBILITY
FRUGALITY	GENEROSITY	GIVING
GRACE	HAPPINESS	HARMONY
HELPFULNESS	HONESTY	HOPEFULNESS
HUMILITY	IMAGINATION	INDEPENDENCE
INGENUITY	INSIGHTFULNESS	INTEGRITY

INTELLIGENCE	INTUITION	JOY
KINDNESS	LOVE	LOYALTY
MODESTY	OPEN-MINDEDNESS	OPTIMISM
PASSION	PEACE	PERSERVERANCE
POWER	PROFESSIONALISM	PUNCTUALITY
REALISM	REASON	RELIABILITY
RESPECT	RESTRAINT	SELF-CONTROL
SENSITIVITY	SINCERITY	SPIRITUALITY
THOROUGHNESS	THOUGHTFULNESS	TRUST
UNDERSTANDING	UNIQUENESS	VIRTUE
WARMTH	WILLINGNESS	WISDOM

The next step is to place a priority on each of the selected values. You may have to think of situations in order to decide the priority of a particular value. Be sure all that appear on your list are truly important to you. Do not rush this exercise; it is important to know the values you use in making decisions and guiding your behavior. List your values in order of importance to you.

1)	9)
2)	10)
3)	11)
4)	12)
5)	13)
6)	14)

7)	15)
8)	

This list can be considered your core beliefs. As you reflect on the words of this list, which of these are qualities coming from your childhood, and which are values that may be more recently valued. Remember, these must be things that are true for you, not what someone else wants to be true for you. It is possible to have a value that is the opposite of something you may have experienced. For example, as a child you may have witnessed discrimination of some type, possibly racial, gender or age. This situation may have created the desire to be totally unlike the actions and behaviors you witnessed. Oftentimes, our values may come from negative experiences and the desire to be different. Your core values should contain thoughts or actions that people will not be able to stop you from doing. These are things that should bring you a sense of accomplishment and satisfaction, pleasure and joy. Orienting your life around the values on this list will allow you to have more of what you would like to have in your life.

One who knows others is wise. One who knows one's self is enlightened.
—Lao Tzu

Importance of Knowing

If you are unclear about your values, you will be unclear about yourself. You may find that you are wandering through life, bouncing from one thing to another in an attempt to find yourself. Your determined list of values is your current compass, showing the direction you are headed. How strongly you believe in your values and how closely you follow them has an effect on how you will live your life. When you choose values that are important to you, and which you strongly believe in, you will move closer to accomplishing your goals and reaching your dreams. Your values help you make important decisions, they help identify people or situations that either support your values (or not), and they help you to know who you are.

If you cannot define yourself by your values, you may find yourself becoming what other people want you or need you to be. There will be little meaning for you from your decisions or your actions. You may even become a non-self. While we believe that our life values reflect our inner being, it is important to take regular reality checks. Are you responding as YOU (standing strong for your convictions), or are you responding as THEM (and compromising your beliefs and values)? Staying focused on your values will insure it is your inner voice that is responsible for your actions and not an external influence. This set of values becomes your being; it is your character.

Character is not reflected by what we say, or even by what we intend. It is a reflection of what we do." —Anonymous

Character

Your character is what you are; it must be developed. The basis for your character comes from your values. There is a consistency between what you *say* you will do, and what it is you *actually* do. Do not confuse your character and your reputation. Your character is **what you are,** and you reputation is **what others say you are.** Abraham Lincoln likened it to a tree and its shadow; the tree is one's character, and the shadow, their reputation.

Whether your character is good or bad depends on the quality of your values. It also depends on your practice of living these values. It is your choice of actions that determines your character. Your habitual way of behaving becomes your character. These are actions you would take even if no one was watching. It is important to care about your reputation, but it is more important to care about your character. A critical part of becoming a person of character is making ethical decisions. Character is ethics in action.

"Action indeed is the sole medium of expression for ethics."
— Jane Addams

Ethics

Ethics and values are not interchangeable. Ethics are how a moral person should behave, while values determine how a person actually behaves. Values relate to ethics based on the beliefs of what is right or wrong. Values are a motivator for ethical behavior. Honesty and truth are values that form the principles for ethical principles. These are the principles that define behavior as right, good and proper. It is not always easy to make ethical decisions. There are social, economic, and professional pressures for types of behaviors that can cloud these decisions. Values can *guide* and *motivate* ethical behavior.

Think about what your reaction is to a situation you feel is unethical or unfair, or just seems wrong to you. Do you turn the other way and avoid the issue, or do you do something to voice your disapproval? To make this decision requires more than just a belief in what is right or wrong. It also requires looking at the choices, analyzing the facts, and being able to evaluate the likely consequences of the choice. The choice for ethical conduct comes from ethical principles based on ethical values.

> *Always do right – this will gratify some and astonish the rest.*
> — Mark Twain

Values In Review

When we make choices and are dissatisfied with the outcome, this is often a result of being disconnected with our values. Values are something we do; they are of value because they are the way we live our lives. Our values are unique to each of us individually. Two people may have similar passions and goals, but very different values. Remember, we have choices! <u>We do not have to live in a manner that is contradictive to our values.</u> In order to live your life in harmony with your values, you must identify them, and then you must keep them in front of you. I suggest you write your list of prioritized values on a note card and put it somewhere where you can see it. Your basic reasons for identifying your values are:

1. In order to be true to yourself, you must know who you are and what you value.

2. You can make decisions easier based upon your values.

3. You can identify the people, situations, and things that you want to have in your life, and those that you do not.

4. It will help you set boundaries for others' behavior; what is acceptable and what is not.

5. It will bring you peace and keep your hopes and dreams alive.

A final exercise in determining your values and the choices you make regarding those values is to take the eulogy test. This is a simple test, but will require some time to deliberate.

Simply answer this question – At your funeral, how would you like your life to be described?

_____

_____

_____

_____

_____

Your answer to this question will tell you if you are on the right path of living your values, or if you need to re-evaluate how you are living your life. Are you living it as YOU? Or are you living it as others expect you to? Only you can determine who is your true self.

"This above all: to thine ownself be true.
And it must follow, as the night the day.
Thou canst not then be false to any man."
— Shakespeare-Hamlet

ABOUT THE AUTHOR

SHARYN LYNN YONKMAN

Sharyn Lynn Yonkman is the founder and principal consultant for Lynn Consulting Group, a personal and professional development training organization. Lynn Consulting specializes in career advancement skills for the professional woman, helping her in achieving personal excellence. As a passionate advocate of women's Self-empowerment and life balance issues, Sharyn offers special expertise in dealing with transition and change in the workplace, as well as programs designed for those of the baby boomer generation.

As former CFO of several high profile retail and hospitality companies, Ms. Yonkman has gained valuable in depth financial and managerial experience in the corporate community providing the knowledge for cost effective solutions for todays business challenges. Training programs available include: Self Projection and Professional Image; Dealing with Change and Embracing Transition; Superior Customer Service in Retail and Hospitality; and Handling Conflict and Fear.

Customized curriculum is offered to meet your specific business needs.

One on one individual life balance coaching is also available.

Born, raised and educated in New Jersey, Sharyn moved to southern California a decade ago. This bi-coastal experience provides her a unique perspective to be able to incorporate the best of each coasts business culture and convey that knowledge to her clients.

Ms. Yonkman is a Co-author of *Remarkable Women*, an anthology project with Marci Shimoff of "The Secret", actress Jennifer O'Neil, and Dottie Walters. Additionally, she is a contributor to *Becoming The Professional Woman* in which she addresses overcoming fear in the workplace and *Overcoming the Superwoman Syndrome*.

She is currently completing a solo project for baby boomer women facing the challenges of moving from the first act of life to the second.

Author, trainer, motivational speaker, and life balance coach, Ms. Yonkman is available internationally to help the individual or organization with their professional developmental needs.

Contact
Lynn Consulting
PO Box 1266
Ventura, Ca 93002
805.677.3117
lynnconsult@yahoo.com
www.protrain.net

EIGHT

CREATING THE LIFE YOU WANT

By Sharyn L. Yonkman

"One must live and create. Live to the point of tears."
—Albert Camus

Are you living the life you truthfully want? Did you know that you have a unique purpose in life, and that you will not be truly happy unless you live it? Life can and should be phenomenal. Is yours?

Success vs. Satisfaction

Success is a relative and very personal concept, and the definition of it can change throughout your life. Personal success is achieved when you feel good about yourself and your significant relationships.

Sometimes your unique purpose in life shows up not as a romanticized dream, but as a vague discontent with yourself and your relationships. Your life may look successful on the outside, but you may be experiencing an indefinable *something* missing. This feeling is your divine dissatisfaction. No matter how successful your life may appear, if you are not living your dream, your sole purpose, you will experience divine dissatisfaction.

Your life purpose is the gift that you, and only you, can give the world. If you are not following your dream, it may be difficult to be motivated or excited about your life and your future. Living your unique purpose can mean the difference between dragging yourself off to do a ho-hum job every day, or awakening each day with great expectations, full of happiness and eager to get to work.

You may not yet know what your life purpose is, but here's a hint: it's probably not the job that leaves you feeling like you have been run over by a bus at days end, or that relationship that leaves you feeling resentful or dead inside. How does your current life match the life you really want?

> *"Dreams come true. Without that possibility, nature would not incite us to have them."* — John Updike

All on Board.

There is a time to leave where you are now, even if there is no sure destination. If you are experiencing divine dissatisfaction, I suggest the time is now. Life is fleeting and finite. Do not delay your happiness. Avoid "I'll be happy when"…thinking. Choose to live a life that makes you feel content. Be happy now.

Finding Your Unique Purpose.

For some of us, our life purpose has been obvious from birth; for most of us, however, discovering it is part of the life journey. In your pursuit of your dreams, you are on the right track if the time spent in this pursuit is enjoyable and feels right. If you are not enjoying the trip, feeling exhausted and unhappy, you are most likely on the wrong track. It is most important to focus on your feelings and stay observant. Remember that even your failures are noteworthy, for they are the learning opportunities that will lead you to the right track.

Exercise
Without thinking or pausing, write down 2-3 dreams that you hold in your heart. They should be dreams of what you want to do and have in your life. Take note if these dreams come to mind easily or not. If so, they might be part of your unique purpose.

_____

_____

_____

_____

_____

Ask yourself what makes you feel motivated and excited, peaceful and content. Trust your instincts and work with your intuition. Always keep an open mind and be alert for signs that appear in a flash, like a sixth sense. Expect your subconscious to show you the way and it will.

What dream would you like to fulfill?

_____

Intuitive Guidance Exercise
Take some quiet time, close your eyes, and take several slow, deep breaths. With a pen and paper at your side, slowly ask yourself the following questions, and be prepared to jot down any thoughts or feelings that come.

- Right now, if I could do anything I wanted to do, it would be _____
  _____

- If I could change anything about myself right now, it would be _____
  _____

- Someday when I am _____ I will be able to _____
  _____

Make a commitment to yourself that **each day this week you will start your day by saying,** "I am awaiting a plan and will follow it when received." **Repeat this often and fasten your seatbelt. You will be moving toward the fast track to your highest potential.**

"People become really remarkable when they start thinking they can do things. When they believe in themselves, they have the first secret of success."
— Norman Vincent Peale

The Secret Is the Law of Attraction.

Universal metaphysical laws show us that thoughts are energy. Thoughts create through attraction. Simply stated, what we think, feel, and believe is what we attract to us. Thoughts become things. You attract to you your dominant thoughts. What you focus on with your thought and feeling is what you attract into your experience.

You are the magnet in the law of attraction. Whatever is going on in your mind is what you are attracting. You need to focus on goals and visions of where you want to be in life because what you focus on is what expands in your life.

Since you already are the magnet, the question is, are you attracting what you want, or more of what you don't want? When you don't like what you have created, turn your attention away from what you don't want and focus on what you do want instead. Send your energy to what you want; never to what you don't want.

If you learn how to control your thoughts and feelings, you can put out your wishes to the universe, like an order in a restaurant, and have your life prepared the way you wish. You are sending out unconscious orders all the times via your thoughts, even if you do not realize it. If you really want the filet mignon, you must stop ordering the burger.

Be aware that, if you project the energy of fear, the universe will respond with more to be afraid of. Fear feeds on attention, so make a concentrated effort not to be afraid. **Decide what it is that you want, believe that you can have it, and believe that you deserve it.**

You have infinite power. When you are full of positive energy and are confident, joyful and grateful, then the law of attraction brings you more for which to be grateful and joyful. Your reality is created by your beliefs, and where your thoughts go, energy flows.

Set your intentions strongly. An intention is the determination to do something, no matter what. Focus on your life purpose and do not lose sight of it.

Your thoughts are the power and energy by which your life experiences are created. There is NOTHING else. Change your thoughts and change your life. It is that simple, and it is that difficult!

There is no sin punished more implacably by nature than the sin of resistance to change" —Anne Morrow Lindbergh (1906-2001)

To Change Your Life, You Must CHANGE YOUR THOUGHTS.

Are your thoughts worthy of you? If not, NOW is the time to change them. Nothing matters but this moment, and what you are focusing your attention on in that moment.

Learn to become still, take your attention away from what you don't want, and instead, place attention on what you do want.

What is it that you REALLY want?

When you have an inspired thought, you must trust and act on it.

Did You Know?

You change your beliefs by replacing them with different ones until the new ones take hold. You can create new brain circuits via this approach. New neural paths are created with repetition. You can do this through the practice of holding on to a vision of the experience you desire, and by creating affirmations that support that vision. Practice makes perfect.

Remember, Thoughts Become Things	
Avoid having these thoughts:	**Instead**, be upbeat, enthusiastic, and say:
"I'm surviving."	"I'm fabulous."
"I'm hanging in there."	"I am feeling great."

Now, in the spaces provided , write down thoughts you typically struggle with and want to change, and replace them with a positive, no limit version.

Avoid	Instead

Be Grateful.

The universe wants you to have what you want, but it also wants you to be grateful for what you have now. Developing an attitude of gratitude is crucial on your journey to creating the life you want. Today, start a gratitude journal. In your journal, list the things you are grateful for. Focus on what you have right now that you are grateful for.

If you are feeling low and negative, this might be very difficult for you at first; you may have to really search for things that inspire gratitude in you. Dig deep, even something as basic as having the eyes to read this, or being grateful for the opportunity to learn this by having this book, will do. As time goes on, I am confident that you will be able to add many things to your gratitude list. Read your list daily and **feel** the gratitude.

A gratitude affirmation: (to be read with the feeling of belief)

I am lucky and grateful to have my life now, and it is just and healthy to desire more.

"Your vision will become clear only when you can look into your heart. Who looks outside, dreams; who looks inside, awakes." — Carl Jung

Awake, create, and visualize your potential for greatness.

A vision is a thought with infinite power to attract the resources for its creation. Your job is to keep the vision fueled with your positive energy. Keep your mind free of thoughts of "how" and keep focused on your vision. Nourish and protect your vision and trust the process. Focus your attention 100% on your vision.

Remember, the purpose of your vision is to bring you Joy. Accept the Joy, because it's all about how you feel. Close your eyes and visualize having what you want and the feeling of already having it. Play the picture in your mind and focus on the end result.

Exercise

Creating Vision Boards: Vision boards are your dream books. They are visual representations of the things you want, and should be kept somewhere where you can view it easily and often. Have fun with this, and don't limit yourself or your dreams.

1. You will need: A large variety of magazines, catalogs, photos and perhaps downloaded web images to collect, pictures that represent the things you want. Tip: include images that look exactly like the things you really want. Remember: these are things YOU want, so don't judge them by the standards of others.

2. Also needed are glue sticks, a poster board and/or scrapbook, colored markers.

3. Suggestions for some areas of inclusion are: Photo of house with surrounding area and furnishings; vacation spots and retreats; desired perfect workspace; automobile; clothes with accessories; your perfect mate (along with engagement & wedding ring).

4. In addition to photos, be sure and included any printed words or phrases that resonate with you and speak to your dreams. Pasting applicable fortunes from cookies over the appropriate images is one example; or you may write messages

with brightly colored markers, as well. As time progresses and your wants change or increase, simply remove the image and replace or add more. There are no limits!

Most importantly, have fun with this exercise and do look at it DAILY.

Create Your Affirmations

Remember that affirmations are simple, present tense statements of what you desire to be true. They implant better beliefs on your subconscious mind. An affirmative thought is much more powerful than a negative one. The words should be emotionalized with your belief in their outcome.

Since gratitude is paramount in engaging the law of attraction, the following should be filled in with your personal belief and repeated daily:

"I am so happy and grateful that_____.

Some other examples you might want to try:

- I am happy with my life right now, and am looking forward to my future.
- I can accomplish anything I want to.
- I am creative and capable.
- I deserve success.
- I know what I want and am motivated to get it.

In spaces below, please write several of your own:

_____

_____

_____

Read these aloud twice a day. Feel and see yourself already in possession of all that you want.

"You don't have to see the whole staircase, just the first step."
— Martin Luther King

DECLARE	→	What you want.
BELIEVE	→	You will get it.
ACT	→	As if you already have it.

Don't Worry About the HOW.

Creating the life you want is always a work in progress. The key to living the life you want is to choose now, in the present moment, to create what you want from your inner self. Do not get stuck worrying about "how" your dreams will manifest. Switch to "what could be possible" thinking. Ask "what" questions, not "how". The universe will take care of the how. You must trust the process and believe you deserve it.

"It's never too late, in fiction or in life, to revise." — Nancy Thayer

Parting Thoughts

Remember when you are working with the laws of attraction to create what you want in life, that it is extremely important that you have fun with the process. If you look at this adventure as yet another job you must do, you will not get the desired results. Take pleasure in the process of creating the life you want and deserve, stay on track, and most of all, ENJOY the ride.

I wish you all a most pleasant journey to your ultimate destinations.

Recommended Resources:

DVD's to view

<u>"What the Bleep Do We Know?" produced by 20th Century Fox home entertainment 2004</u>

"The Secret" produced by Rhonda Byrne <u>www.thesecret.tv</u>. (TIP: There are two editions. If you can, get the original one, which includes Esther Hicks.)

Books

The Law of Attraction by Esther and Jerry Hicks, Hay House 2006

The Life Audit: A Step-By-Step Guide to Taking Stock, Gaining Control, and Creating the Life You Want by Caroline Righton, Broadway Books 2006

Ask and It Is Given: Learning to Manifest Your Desires by Abraham (Spirit), Hay House 2004

This Year I Will...How to Finally Change a Habit, Keep a Resolution, or Make a Dream Come True by M. J. Ryan, Broadway Books 2006

The Secret by Rhonda Byrne, ATRIA Books 2006

ABOUT THE AUTHOR

Ahmon'dra (Brenda) McClendon

Ahmon'dra, President of Brilliance Inc., is an international speaker, facilitator, motivator and author. She imprints an indelible impression upon your heart and makes you smile, laugh, cry and contemplate the deeper issues of life. She arouses in each listener a passion to commit to his or her higher purpose with her grace, power and spirit.

With twenty plus years in the human services arena and an MSW from San Francisco State University, Ahmon'dra has developed a highly successful program called P.L.A.N.E. – "Passionately Living A New Existence." She has spoken to thousands of young adults in North America, Europe and Africa on how to create a powerful future by staying devoted to their dreams, trusting their intuition, boldly taking risks and asking for what they want.

She is a Certified Facilitator for Motivating the Teen Spirit Inc. a teen empowerment program that conducts transformational workshops, and leads the international program, Core Value Training as a Senior Instructor. Ahmon'dra is a recipient of the "Speaking with an Active Voice" grant sponsored by the American Medical Women's Association and Pharmacia Corporation.

A contributing author to the best selling book *Chicken Soup For the African-American Soul*, she was featured as a keynote speaker for The Monster Diversity 2003 Leadership Program in the United States.

Passion and magnificence exude from her presence with an amazing energy of wisdom, healing & love as she creates, flies and soars! Get clear on your life and passions with the energy and excitement of Ahmon'dra

Contact
Ahmon'dra (Brenda) McClendon
Brilliance, Inc.
484 Lakepark Ave pmb 485
Oakland, California 94610
Ahmondra@aol.com
www.protrain.net

NINE

OVERCOMING ANGER AND BITTERNESS

By Ahmon'dra McClendon

It takes Courage to eliminate anger and bitterness from life! Having the ability to overcome these emotions <u>before</u> they turn deadly gives us the freedom to live life fully.

Understanding that pain in life is mandatory, but suffering is optional and provides us with a choice. We either feel the pain and move through it, or create fear and suffer in it.

When we perceive a threat to our existence, we experience an internal disturbance called "Fear". Depending on our capabilities, we either resolve the fear, or repress it. If we resolve the fear, we move forward in life. If we repress the fear, we get stuck, and our life fills with anger and bitterness. These two emotions left unchecked can develop into rage.

Children don't have the cognitive ability to resolve their fears, and so they hide them in their unconscious. If these are normal childhood fears, they get resolved in time. However, when abuse (physical, emotional, sexual) or intimidation is present during childhood, the amount of hidden unresolved fears never reaches resolution. Instead, they get carried into adulthood, and create the perfect breeding ground for anger and bitterness.

The extreme outcomes of unresolved fear and repressed anger are acute destructive behaviors, such as suicide (rage turned inward) or homicide (rage turned outward). The majority of us don't advance to rage; we stop at chronic anger.

Our whole way of thinking, feeling, and behaving is clouded by anger. We become resentful of others who look happy. This creates frustration, which creates bitterness, which flows into anger. We want to stop this vicious cycle, but don't know how.

My Personal Journey

After living years in an abusive environment, the anger and bitterness embedded in my personal life finally exploded into rage. I was forced to end my self-imposed isolation and seek help. Up to that point, any happiness I had was only an illusion. My life appeared to be good from a distance, but upon closer examination the imprint of my anger was unmistakable. I lived in constant fear of my own anger, not knowing what to expect if I lost my temper. People didn't want to be in my company because it was painful. The bold ones dared to ask, "Why are you always so angry?" or "Do you ever have anything positive to say?" My reply was always a vicious snap or lethal verbal swipe.

I was just as much in the dark as they were about my condition. My life-long questions were, "Why am I so angry" and "Why am I always seething with bitterness?" I felt trapped, and had resigned myself to living a life of loneliness and solitude. I didn't just feel anger and bitterness. <u>I *was* anger and bitterness.</u>

After years of searching for answers, I discovered there was nothing wrong with me. My anger and bitterness had developed as defense mechanisms to help me survive the harsh environment I grew up in. Unfortunately, they continued to operate past their usefulness, and what was once helpful to me became a hindrance.

When my internalized fear was resolved the door to spiritual growth opened and I was free to experience true happiness. My anger and bitterness no longer stood in my way.

Overcoming anger and bitterness is a process. It is a journey that can only be taken one step at a time. It is my intention in this chapter to:

- Identify how anger is manifesting in your life.

- Trace the source of the anger by exposing the underlying fears.

- Outline techniques to resolve your anger

The Roadmap to Freedom: The Pathway Through Anger and Bitterness.

Step #1: The Start: Where Are You Right Now?
What part does anger play in your life today?

_____

_____

What part does bitterness play in your life today?

_____

_____

Make a list of triggers that provoke your anger?

_____

_____

What do you do to manage your anger?

_____

_____

What are the symptoms of chronic anger/bitterness?

_____

_____

Identify the impact your anger/bitterness is having on your:
- Physical Life: _____
- Emotional Life: _____
- Spiritual Life: _____
- Social Life: _____
- Financial Life: _____

How do you express angry feelings?

_____

_____

Do you struggle not to lose your temper?

_____

_____

Do you ever lose control of your temper? If so, how intense does it get?

_____

_____

Are you ever fearful about your angry reactions toward others?

_____

_____

Describe how your biological family members expressed their anger:
- Family member #1: _____
- Family member #2: _____
- Family member #3: _____
- Family member #4: _____

How has their behavior affected your life?
- Affect from family member #1: _____
- Affect from family member #2: _____
- Affect from family member #3: _____
- Affect from family member #4: _____

Are you still haunted by childhood fears? Share your feelings.

_____

_____

_____

_____

_____

_____

Step #2—The Journey: In What Direction Are You Growing?

Let's examine the direction your anger takes. Once you know the direction, you can take steps to eliminate the anger, and change the direction of your life.

There are degrees of feelings and degrees of emotions. Losing your temper and having an argument is not the same as losing your temper and going into a blind rage. The intensity of anger and bitterness affects all aspects of life and blocks happiness. It can manifest as depression, extreme fatigue, or disrupt sleeping and eating patterns. When we understand the depth of our anger, we can manage it.

The growth of anger and bitterness can be compared to the growth of a tree. A tree begins as a seed and develops according to the blueprint within it. When the seed is properly cared for, it grows into a strong healthy tree. The process is the same for chronic anger. The blueprint for anger is within every experience of fear or pain. If the pain or fear isn't resolved, it will grow into anger and bitterness. With the proper environment (abusive or isolated), it will develop roots (feelings of deep hurt), a trunk (negative disposition), branches (toxic emotions) and leaves (damaging behaviors). It will eventually sprout and populate the surrounding areas (an angry person can create an angry family). No two trees are identical; however, one technique can be applied to cut them down. Chronic anger and bitterness can also be overcome using the same techniques.

Cutting the Tree of Toxic Anger:

1. The leaves and branches are cut back. *Toxic emotions and destructive behaviors are eliminated.*

List the toxic emotions/behavior you want to eliminate.

- _____
- _____
- _____

2. The trunk is cut into small pieces. *The negative attitudes are replaced.*

List the negative attitudes you want to replace.

- _____
- _____

3. The roots are then uprooted. *An inventory of childhood fears and pain is completed.*

List the fears you repressed in childhood and carried into adulthood

- _____
- _____

Step #3—The Destination (Where Do You Want To Be?)

Create another list of the emotions and behaviors you want to exhibit.

- _____
- _____

Exercise: Your Personal Collage

Purchase a poster board in your favorite color and, using cut outs from magazines, create a collage that shows the new positive attitude, behaviors, and feelings you want to express. Display your masterpiece proudly. Let it represent your road map to happiness. (Review your list of the new emotions you want to exhibit.)

Surround yourself with positive images, and remember: Pain in life is mandatory, but suffering is optional!

Recommended Reading

Overcoming Emotional Chaos by Doc Childre & Deborah Rozman 2002

Authority Overrides Power by 2003 Barbara Perkins

The Secret DVD 2006

Chicken Soup for The African American Soul, 2005

ABOUT THE AUTHOR

ROSEMARY BONILLA

Rosemary Bonilla currently resides in Staten Island, New York with her husband and two children aged twenty and thirteen. She has over twenty years experience in the healthcare industry with ten years at a management level and is currently pursuing a Master's Degree in Health Administration. She has taught Medical Billing/Coding at Wagner College in Staten Island, New York. Ms. Bonilla is president and CEO of the profitable medical billing company, president and CEO of a real estate holding company, as well as a practice manager for the Department of Radiology at Maimonides Medical Center.

She holds memberships with the New York State Real Estate Association, National Association of Female Executives, Radiology Business Management Association, Medical Group Management Association, New Day Toastmasters, Fellow in the American College of Medical Practice Executives, and is an International Advisory Board member of The Professional Woman Network.

Rosemary Bonilla is a Certified Trainer in personal and professional development and conducts seminars and workshops nationally and internationally specializing in developing a positive self-image, financial freedom and personal and professional development. She is also available for personal and professional coaching sessions.

Contact:
Rosemary Bonilla
Faculty Practice Manager
Radiology Department
Maimonides Medical Center
4802 Tenth Avenue
Brooklyn, NY 11219
(718) 283-6157
rbonilla@maimonidesmed.org
www.protrain.net

TEN

LIVING A JOYFUL LIFE

By Rosemary Bonilla

"Happiness depends more on the inward disposition of mind than on outward circumstances."—Benjamin Franklin

If we are to become joyful, we must set ourselves apart to a given purpose or occasion that is a source for positive emotions and gratification. We should be genuine to ourselves and ask, "What brings me joy?" Surely the answers to that question are different for everyone, as we must be true to our authentic self. But a key for each person to begin embracing joy is to become **grateful.** Learning to be content in all circumstances and situations (even the hard ones) brings joy. It is because of adversity that change and healing come, learning to recognize that without adversity we would not grow, and that growth and healing is part of the process of becoming joyful and content. Having a mission or purpose in life, helping others, and knowing that our mission or purpose is to serve others truly, can lead to a joy-filled life. Appreciating the little things in life that are free, such as good health, clean air, a smiling face, and a baby's laughter, can bring abounding joy. And finally, the biggest ingredient for joy is **LOVE;** not conditional, but **UNCONDITIONAL** love, for ourselves and others.

Many years ago, Thomas Jefferson revealed to us the American Dream. *"Life, liberty and the pursuit of happiness"* is the secret motive that drives many women. Researchers have found that happy people tend to:

• Have high self-esteem.

• Be optimistic, outgoing and agreeable.

• Have close friendships or a satisfying marriage.

• Have work and leisure that engage their skills.

• Have a meaningful religious faith.

• Sleep well and exercise.

However, happiness may or may not be affected by the following: it depends upon the attitude of the individual as to whether they will or will not be happy given these circumstances:

• Age

• Gender

• Education level

• Parenthood

• Physical attractiveness

What Brings You a Joy?

Stop and think for a moment:

What is the most joyful event that you have ever experienced?

_____

_____

What emotional needs were met by that joyful experience?

1. _____
2. _____
3. _____
4. _____
5. _____

This study was conducted by Ed Diener and Martin Seligman with university students; the top three emotions were self-esteem, feeling connected with others (relatedness), and autonomy (feeling in control). At the bottom of the list of less satisfaction-predicting factors was money and luxury.

Does Money Buy Happiness?

Most people agree that money cannot buy happiness. Since 1957, the average American buying power more than doubled due partly to women's increasing employment. This has bought us twice as many cars, televisions, laptops, air conditioners and cell phones; but did this buy us happiness? More money helps us to avoid certain types of pain, but since our buying power more than doubled, it is reported that the average American's **happiness has remained unchanged.** *If you are focusing on what you have instead of* **who you are**, you will never feel satisfied and never experience lasting joy. Joy comes from defining and developing your whole self!! What is the point of striving for "stuff" if it does not lead to the joyful, good life? The prophet Isiah from the Old Testament wondered, "*Why do you spend your money for that which is not bread, and your labor for that which does not satisfy?*" What is the point of accumulating luxury cars, yachts, bigger homes, more CD's, closets full of unworn clothes, leaving a significant amount of wealth to one's heirs (as if it could buy them happiness) rather than applying it to a hurting world? We are not happier because of our affluent wealth since 1957; in fact, the number of Americans who say they are "very happy" has declined from 35% to 32 %. Meanwhile, the divorce rate has nearly quadrupled (even after the recent decline) since 1957, and more people than ever (especially teens and young adults) are depressed. We are a generation of pill-popping, anti-depressant Americans. Our affluent wealth is soaring, but we are poor in spirit! More than ever before in history we have bigger houses but broken homes, higher incomes but lower morals, secured rights but diminished civility. We strive for a higher income, which we think will give us a higher lifestyle, but aim low at making a life. We celebrate prosperity, but yearn for purpose. We cherish our freedom, but yearn to be autonomous.

What do you value, that money cannot buy?
1. _____
2. _____
3. _____
4. _____

What are you passionate about?
1. _____
2. _____
3. _____

If you inherited a million dollars, what would you do with it? Would it make you happy? Why?

1 _____

2. _____

3. _____

4. _____

What have you done to bring joy to another human being that cost nothing:

1. _____

2. _____

3. _____

4. _____

Comparing Ourselves to Others

Unfortunately, we are always comparing ourselves to others and trying to "keep up with the Joneses". As we reach for the ladder of success, we often compare ourselves with our peers who are at (or above) our rung on the ladder. Napoleon envied Caesar, Caesar envied Alexander, and Alexander envied Hercules (who never existed). There will always be someone who is more successful than you are! When we compare ourselves to others, we create envy, which is a negative destructive emotion that will never give us joy, but instead, **more grief**. So what do we do when envy rears its ugly head? **We must count our blessings!** Remember, the first key in becoming joyful is being *grateful*. Remember the old Persian saying, "I cried because I had no shoes until I met a man who had no feet." So be ever grateful, and remember to be thankful every day for the solace of little delights and **gifts that are given to us for free** (a hug, a beautiful sunset, the warm breeze, the ocean, a loved one recovering from cancer, kindness, and the love of your child).

Pleasure

If your current condition (whether it is your income, social prestige or grade point average) increases, you will feel a surge of pleasure. But once this surge of pleasure subsides, we must have a new level of achievement for another "pleasure surge", and on and on it goes! When I was growing up, we were satisfied with one television set in our home, but now we feel deprived if there is not one in every room of our house. Our adaptation level increases, which explains why, despite realities of triumph and tragedy, million dollar lottery winners and people who are paralyzed report roughly similar levels of joy. Seeking happiness through material achievement requires an ever-increasing accumulation of stuff. To feel gratified, our achievements must surpass our expectations. Satisfying tasks and relationships affect our happiness, but always within the limits driven by our genetic makeup. A study done by David Lykken Auke Tellegen estimated that 50% of the difference among people's happiness rating is inherited. Depending on our level of self-esteem and recent experiences, our happiness fluctuates around a *set point,* which is the reason by some people are always upbeat and others down trodden. But, even though you are genetically influenced, you can change your levels of joy!

Here are some suggestions for improving your mood and satisfaction with life:

1. Realize that enduring happiness doesn't come from financial success.

2. Take control of your time.

3. Act happy.

4. Seek work and leisure that engages your skills and talents.

5. Eat right and exercise regularly.

6. Get enough sleep.

7. Make your relationships number one in your life.

8. Help others.

9. BE GRATEFUL.

10. Feed your spiritual self.

I feel that the greatest benefit of the "Dot Boom to Dot Bust" era will turn out to be that more people experienced great wealth at a very early age than ever before in history, and due to this, there are among us a very large amount of people who know the emptiness that comes from fast cars, easy love, and big empty houses. But, there are a lot of smart young people out there today who are dedicated (more than ever) to making a difference and not a dollar. They know, at least in the deepest way, that money does not buy happiness.

Four Qualities That Bring Joy.
1. **A sense of purpose or mission.** What really "drives" you?
   - _____
   - _____
   - _____

2. **Serving Others:** List ways in which you serve others.
   - _____
   - _____
   - _____

3. **Gratitude for the free things in life.** What are they?

- _____
- _____
- _____

4. **Unconditional loving relationships.** You do you love unconditionally?

- _____
- _____
- _____

We are entering a new era with increasing concern for relationships and not materialism. If materialism does not create happiness, then let us look at the major ingredients that do!

1. **Close, supportive relationships.** Those that have intimate friendships or committed satisfying marriages are much happier.

2. **Faith communities.** In a National Opinion Research Center survey of 42,000 Americans since 1972, 26% of those rarely or never attending religious services declared themselves very happy, as did 47% percent of those attending multiple times monthly.

3. **Positive traits.** Optimism, self-esteem, and autonomy of one's life are the traits that mark happy experiences and happy lives. Happy people are empowered people. They have control of their lives. They are not victims, but victors. They know they have the power to control their thoughts, words, emotions, actions, and experiences, which will eventually control their destiny.

4. **Purpose and flow.** This is someone who knows what they want. They have goals, and love what they do. They are engaged in a

position that utilizes their skills and talent. They have balance between their work and leisure. They are not overwhelmed or stressed out, or "underwhelmed" and bored. They are engaged in an activity that brings purpose to their lives. They may lose consciousness of time as they focus on their vision, mission, and purpose. They often feel deep fulfillment from serving others.

Becoming joyful is attainable. Things that make up a genuinely good life can be controlled by you and are enduringly sustainable. We should strive for a new vision of a unified dream for all people that does not have to destroy our economy or people, but will require a new season. A season that can not only be laced with prosperity, but also with purpose to help each other; capital with compassion, which leads to empathy for others, and enterprise with freedom to create autonomous lives. Such a transformation of universal consciousness has happened before in our lifetime! (Think about the way America felt about race, gender, and the environment fifty years ago.) Choose to be joyful, do what you love, be grateful for what you have, and stop comparing your blessings to others. Be your own best friend, strive to give the best service to others, and expect a good reward for it. Be of good cheer, and overcome by knowing who you are. Joy is sustainable; embrace it.

Happiness Quotes
Success is getting what you want. Happiness is liking what you get.
—H. Jackson Brown

Talk happiness. The world is sad enough without your woe.
—Orison Sweet Marden

The best way for a person to have a happy thought is to count his blessings, not his cash. —Anonymous

The best way for a person to cheer up is to try to cheer somebody else up —Mark Twain

A man's life is what his thoughts make of it. —Marcus Aurelius

You're happiest while you're making the greatest contribution —John F. Kennedy

Happiness depends upon ourselves. —Aristotle

To be happy, we must not be too concerned with others. —Albert Camus

No man is happy who does not think himself so. —Publilius Syrus

A pessimist sees the difficulty in opportunity, and an optimist sees the opportunity in every difficulty. —Winston Churchill

Be happy while you are living, for you're long time dead. —Scottish Proverb

Notes:

_____

_____

_____

_____

_____

_____

_____

_____

_____

_____

_____

_____

_____

_____

_____

_____

_____

_____

_____

_____

ABOUT THE AUTHOR

THERESA DOZIER-DANIEL

Theresa Dozier-Daniel is president and founder of Kingdom Ambassador Outreach Ministries/Women of Essence, a training and personal enhancement company. She specializes in the areas of empowering individuals to fulfill God's original plan and purpose for their lives. Theresa's focuses on personal growth through gaining confidence in one own abilities. Learning how to view you through the word of God, Her motto is "I can do all things through God that gives me strength".

Her own story is one of how a person can overcome great difficulties in life to become a survivor.

She has served various faith-based organizations, hospitals, social-services agencies, through facilitation, keynote presentations, workshops, training, consulting, conferences, women retreats, , and other special events. Theresa has facilitated workshops on life skills, self-esteem, cultural diversity, conflict resolution, chemical dependency/alcohol tobacco and gender specific issues.

She is an ordained minister, author, counselor and senior adjunct professor at Burlington County College. Theresa has over twenty-five years of professional experiences dealing with the social ills of our society mental health, addiction, criminal justice and domestic violence.

Theresa holds certifications and professional membership in the following organizations:

- Board Certified Professional Christian Counselor American Association of Christian Counselors
- National Association of Forensic Counselors
- The American College of Certified Forensic Counselors
- Masters of Addiction Counselor
- Domestic Violence Counselor
- National Assoc of Female Executive
- Delta Sigma Theta Sorority

Theresa holds a Master of Science degree in Counseling and a Bachelor of Arts degree in Psychology.

She is an advocate for women and children's rights. Theresa has a strong desire to bring women together where topics and relevant issues is discussed and knowledge is shared to address needs that are of importance to them such as health/wellness, economic advancement of women, women in business, advancement in education, violence, and justice…

Theresa Dozier-Daniel is the Author of *The Hidden Hand of God.*

Contact
Women of Essence
P.O. Box 2462
Cinnamison, NJ.08077
(609) 280-2866
Tdozierdaniel@verizon.net

ELEVEN

FROM VICTIM TO SURVIVOR

By Theresa Dozier-Daniel

*"The greatest glory of living lies in never falling,
but in rising every time you fall."*—Nelson Mandela

The life of Nelson Mandela is very inspiring to me; his life represented an individual with a spirit of determination. He turned a challenging, appalling incident in his nation into a **life** cause. It defined him as a champion, a man of integrity, and one of the most admired figures of our age. Mandella was a Time Man of the Year in 1993. In a BBC television interview with commentator Brian Walden, Mandela stated that he is not a messiah, just an ordinary man who became a leader because of extraordinary circumstances. **A person of character always arises in the midst of a difficult situation.**

Nelson Mandela was born in South Africa, and after his father's death he was raised by a powerful relative. He avoided an arranged marriage and a comfortable life style to take up the cause of democratic nonviolent revolution against apartheid. Because of his stand against apartheid, he was incarcerated for twenty-seven years in Robben Island Prison.

Mandela made good use of a "bad situation"; during his time of incarceration he organized "Island University", where the inmates were able to study subjects such as philosophy, history, politics, literature, economics, etc. In 1989, he began to negotiate with the government for his release. In 1990, *he became the first democratically elected President of South Africa. It was a history-making event.*

I am sure that Nelson Mandela had to struggle with the negative emotions of rage, grief, bitterness, and the thoughts of revenge. The very thought of doing twenty-seven years in prison would surely be an overwhelming ordeal! I believe that he had to dig deep down inside of himself and pull out survival skills and wisdom that he learned from his African heritage. (In order to survive a crisis, you have to break the problem into bite-size pieces.

I am sure that he focused on getting through one day at a time, not all twenty-seven years at once.)

Nelson Mandela faced a negative situation that could have paralyzed him with fear, resentment, and caused him to go into mental isolation, but he continue to be an advocate inside of the prison system. He poured himself into a greater cause that he was passionate about: **education.** He worked on organizing the university at the prison where inmates could have an opportunity to learn and grow. (It's very therapeutic in nature to reach outside of your pain and assist someone else that may be less fortunate than you.)

Even though Mandela was physically in prison, he was mentally liberated. **The walls and bars of obstacles cannot imprison a person that chooses to be unbound in their thinking.**

Our mental attitudes dictate how we respond to people, and even situations. You have a choice as to which attitude you will adopt. If you feel upset and angry about something that happens, that is how you choose to feel. The event itself does not dictate to you how you *should* feel. Sometimes we allow circumstance in our life to influence how we feel.

You can choose to be happy, in spite of what is going on in your life. ***Nelson Mandela survived against all odds and so can you.***

Lessons to Be Learned

We have to learn to *transform obstacles into opportunities for us. Start looking for the good in the midst of complexity, and what lessons you can learn that would be of a great value to you, and that you can eventually share with others. The lesson is to take the focus off of ourselves and reflect on finding the solution.* Seek a valuable lesson in every adversity. Allow the incident to change you for the better. This process can take some time and patience because it will require a shift in your thought processes. This is inner healing restorative type of work.

Exercise

What challenges and obstacles in life have turned into opportunities for you?

1. _____

2. _____

3. _____

Being a Victim is an Attitude of Our Mind.

Let's say something unpleasant has happened to you or a family member. Perhaps you have been abused through rape, domestic violence, incest, molestation, a bad relationship, or deceived by a business associate. You might get angry; you will certainly feel violated by what really has happened to you. Oftentimes, the "victim" feels that it was their fault, and that they brought the problem/abuse on themselves. Why do we allow ourselves to embrace that thought and feeling? We take hold onto this like a life jacket!

Yet, this feeling of being a victim is not a life jacket because it really becomes our **anchor** and eventually keeps us from moving ahead into forgiveness and a survivor mentality. We stay in one place without growing; always placing blame, feeling rage, and oftentimes self-guilt.

If we have something done to us, we are victims, but we do not have to stay there! If we physically survive, we are survivors. Where there is life, there is HOPE to continue on.

Sadly, many never travel any further. They remain psychological, emotional, or spiritual prisoners in moments of history. *To become a victor is to move from being an object of history to becoming a subject/human being once more.*

Exercise
List events that have happened in your history when you have been a victim:
1. _____
2. _____
3. _____

Do you have a victim mentality about those events? You may say NO! That is not me! But spend some time reflecting and really think about it. There are advantages to being a victim. The most appealing is all of the attention/pity that you will get from family and friends; and if you are a victim, you do not ever have to be liable for anything in your life. After all, nothing is your fault because you are the injured party. I call this the –

"Victim Excuse"!

Let's look at the excuses of the individual with "Victim Mentality:

- It is not my fault that I can't keep a job; after all my dad could never keep one."

- "My parents didn't give me enough love; they didn't tuck me into bed at night, and read me bedtime stories."

- "I had a horrible childhood. My parents fought all the time, and that is why I can't stay committed in a relationship. It is not my fault that I cheated on my spouse. I have never seen a good marriage. So what do you expect from me?"

- "It is not my fault that I drink too much; my dad was an alcoholic. I have a disease, and I am powerless in the face of my addiction."

- "Nobody loves me, my spouse hates me, the kids disrespect me, the dog bit me, my friends don't understand me." (It can go on and on.)

Take Back Your Life.

A person that holds a victim mentally will always blame everything and anything on outside circumstances. If this is done often enough, it will become a way of life for you. It is a rather sad, empty and gloomy way to live. This is victimization! You became a helpless person.

It's time to take responsibility for your action and take your life back! **You can choose** the way that you feel. Life for you will become so much richer and take on new meaning if you shed the "victim mentality" (the Why Me Syndrome) and move into the "survivor mentality". (The 'It Happened to Me, But I Am Strong Again' Syndrome.)

The child who survives an abusive situation is extremely courageous, strong, and self-reliant. The woman, who has come out of a horrible relationship and can keep on going, is powerful beyond belief. The single mother who brings home the bacon, cooks it, and raises the children (not skipping a beat) is to be greatly admired. The person that can forgive another individual (even after feeling violated) has a beautiful heart, and so much to offer the world around them. The human spirit is so powerful and can rejuvenate after pain and abuse! We are powerful above measure, because we are created in the image of God.

Forgiveness

The key to making movement in your life is **"letting go and walking in forgiveness"** toward others, as well as yourself. It is not easy at first, but once you release the person that has wounded you, it's very freeing for you. Why? Because YOU are no longer carrying the baggage of the pain. You will know when you are totally healed and restored because you will be able to talk about the situation without the sting of the pain tormenting you.

Exercise

Who have you forgiven?

1. _____
2. _____
3. _____

Rebuilding Your Life

To build a new, strong survivor mentality, it is time to take good care of your emotions, mind, and relationships. Consider the following:

- Have a positive attitude of faith. Mark 9:23, states, *"All things are possible for those who believe."*

- Take time out for YOU; make personal time for rest, relaxation and reflection. Rest not only restores the body, but the mind, as well. *Learn to love yourself.*

- Create and build positive relationships, and avoid critics and negative individuals, as they are toxic and will deplete and drain you. Reach out to others–find new, positive connections.

- Know your limitations, change what you can, and have the wisdom to know the difference.

- Create a healthy balance in your life between work and recreation.

- Celebrate little victories along the way.

- Break your problems/ challenges into bite-size pieces.

- Look at the problem as an opportunity to learn and grow; view impossible situation as opportunities for learning/growth.

- Consider getting outside of the box–make changes, as change disrupts our comfort zone.

- Identify some of the feelings that will surface when we face changes in our lives, such as fear and anger.

- Learn to accept change; be inquiring/inquisitive, discover new interests.

- Be assured that "this too shall pass".

- Meet each new challenge with hope and realistic optimism.

- Approach adversity/stress with a sense of hope.

- Thinking critically and reflectively.

- Belief and purpose propel you forward into life with great possibilities.

- Know what you believe in.

- Get a clear vision of what you want and desire.

- Be flexible and shift gears, if necessary.

- Our strength must be in God, not in ourselves; this takes us out of the driver's seat.

- Manage your emotions; be calm, and at peace with yourself and your surroundings.

- Push beyond your discomfort.

- You will survive your wilderness experience; it is not designed to kill you.

- The only way out of a problem is through it.

- Learn to laugh at yourself. Humor plays a big part.

The following is a very powerful prayer. I know that it is attached to fabric of the AA fellowship and has impacted many lives; it is called The Serenity Prayer.

"God grant us the serenity to accept the things we cannot change,
courage to change the things we can,
and wisdom to know the difference."

The following quotes were written by some of the world's most famous people. I hope that as you read these words of wisdom, they will inspire, challenge, and motivate you to never ever give up.

- *In the middle of difficulty lies opportunity.* —Albert Einstein

- *A pessimist sees the difficulty in every opportunity; an optimist sees the opportunity in every difficulty.* —Sir Winston Churchill

- *If you are going through hell, keep going.* —Sir Winston Churchill

- *Many are the afflictions of the righteous, BUT the Lord delivers them out of them all.* —Holy Bible

- *You gain strength, courage, and confidence by every experience in which you really stop to look fear in the face. You must do the thing you think you cannot do.* —Eleanor Roosevelt

- *People are always blaming their circumstances for what they are. I don't believe in circumstance. The people who get on in the world are the people who get up and look for the circumstances they want, and if they can't find them, make them.* —George Bernard Shaw, Irish playwright

- *Success is not final. Failure is not fatal. It is the courage to continue that makes the difference.* —Winston Churchill

No matter what you have been through in life, whether it was abuse, unkindness, a shattered relationship, or personal failure, it is vital to shed the victim role. You are a survivor. Release yourself from the burden of guilt or anger and step into a new life of forgiveness and self-love.

Recommended Reading

The Hidden Hand of God by Theresa Dozier-Daniel

Tough Times Never Last, But Tough People Do by Robert Schuller

Naomi's Breakthrough Guide by Naomi Judd

Notes:

ABOUT THE AUTHOR

ELIZABETH M. WATERBURY, P.E., P.P., C.M.E.

Elizabeth Waterbury is the President and founder of E. M. Waterbury & Associates Consulting Engineers, a successful Consulting Engineering firm specializing in Land Use and Land Use Development. The focus of her career is to provide quality professional engineering services with a commitment to innovation and personal attention. Ms. Waterbury's firm consists of a talented group of female professionals and support staff who have made their mark in this specialized field of engineering, which is highly competitive and dominated by larger engineering firms.

When not working in her firm, Ms. Waterbury mentors others in professionalism, leadership and balance. This is accomplished through her many and diverse roles that vary from university professor to providing speeches as a member of The Professional Woman International Speakers Bureau. Her unique ability to channel her technical mind into creative and down-to-earth communication allows her to mentor to a broad range of individuals. One of her most honored rolls was to be the keynote speaker for the Southwest Regional Conference for the Society of Woman Engineer's. She has also been honored as a member of the International Advisory Board for The Professional Woman Network since 1990.

Her most cherished role is that of mother. She has worked hard since her daughter's birth to raise her daughter while running her firm. She is well versed in the difficulties that face women who wish to pursue their career, as well as be active in their family's lives. Her message of balance, defining personal success, and personal empowerment is carried through in all of her endeavors.

Contact
Elizabeth Waterbury, P.E., P.P., C.M.E.
E. M. Waterbury & Associates, P.A.
17 Monmouth Street
Red Bank, NJ 07701
(732) 747-6530
Fax (732) 747-6778
EMWAssoc@aol.com
www.protrain.net

TWELVE

LIVING WITH CHRONIC ILLNESS

By Elizabeth Waterbury

I never thought years ago that I would be in the position to have *five* phone numbers associated with just me; *ten* total for our immediate family (all with call waiting), just waiting for me to do my best at multi-tasking. In today's technology, we are called to do more, faster, and all at one time. But there is one flaw in the technology – it's all connected to Me! I may have two ears, but they are tied to one brain and one mouth.

I had prided myself at keeping it all together, sorted and organized. Bring it on! I loved to do many things, in a wide variety, and usually all at once. I had a great memory. Remembering numbers and facts was my forte. I am a civil engineer and we are called to be super-people who can stay sharp and accurate with very little sleep, and when all hell is breaking loose.

One day about five years ago, I got a phone call from my doctor telling me that I had Lyme Disease and a co-infection of Chronic Mono. I laughed. "How could that be? Do you know how much I do in a day? If I had all that, you would think that I would not be able to get out of bed!" I ran my own company, took care of my family, including my four-year-old who had been sick on and off since she was four days old, and I co-shared the responsibility of taking care of my elderly aunt and her disabled son. Shortly before that, I had added college teaching at the local university into the mix. (As an aside–yes, I am one of the authors in the "*Overcoming the Superwoman Syndrome*" book in this series.)

I quickly learned that I had a disease that was not acknowledged by most of the medical community as being one that could be chronic. That meant that I had an uphill battle to fight to get myself treated. I missed my daughter's first day of kindergarten, and went for several weeks out to Kansas City, Missouri to get IV treatments. Since I was in denial about the reality of what I had, I figured I would return home in two weeks and be ready to jumped right back on that crazy train. I had no idea how crazy it was about to get....

The interesting thing is that I did not even know I was sick. I had gone out to the doctor with my sister and my daughter as last resorts with their illnesses. I had known this physician, Carol Ann Ryser, M.D. for years, and knew she was someone with special talents. I had exhausted all local measures first in attempting to find help for my daughter. I videotaped my daughter having her extreme coughing fits that would cause her to throw up and turn purple. They would last for hours. Her poor little stomach would hurt from the violent coughing. Not one local New Jersey doctor would look at the tape. They would just put her on new medicine to treat the symptoms. No one searched for the cause. When she was on *seven* medicines with three of them being steroids, and yet there was no improvement, I said – STOP! I am not doing this any more. This is not making sense. **That's when we all went west on the trip that changed our lives forever.**

One day, nearly twenty years ago, a little bug about the size of a pin head took a ride on my skin and then left without being noticed. I did not notice a mark. I did not notice a bite. I was not unfamiliar with ticks, as I had removed many over the years. It was part of my nature to be outside, and it was part of my profession to be in the woods and in undeveloped areas. I shared this information with Dr. Carol Ann Ryser in Missouri, as she had asked about tick bites as I learned later that my entire family had **Lyme Disease**, which can be spread by ticks.

Last summer we had my daughter in Kansas City for ten weeks of IV treatments, after we learned that she had Lyme Disease. My husband and I were afraid that it would be a negative experience for her, so it felt very bold when we decided to do it. It was hard. The separation was difficult, as my husband stayed in New Jersey and came to visit us when he could. But we've come to learn that life is full of experiences. All experiences have a gift to offer. We met wonderful people. My daughter added a spark of life for the adults getting treatment with us. We did what we could and made the best of each day as well we could. We returned and it is now a past chapter. My daughter learned how to try something different and to take a risk. She learned how to get by in a place that was not home. She also learned that being a kid is important, as you have so much to offer others. We left our friends with coloring books and hope. We also learned that, no matter what your age, you can make a difference by just doing the best that you can, and always being willing to help others the best you can, even if it is just with a smile, a hug, or a colorful picture.

Chronic disease does not just affect the one person who has it. It affects all that are around them. It is hard to watch others suffer and know that there is little you can do. Modern technology leaves us all thinking that we can take a pill for anything and it will be cured. We have become a people that do not have the patience and the push to tough it out. Whether we like it or not, we deteriorate from what we could do before. There is no cure for aging. It can be slowed. But it cannot be stopped. I have been through many stages while living with my disease. I have been through the stage of believing this is only temporary (my definition of the time frame associated with temporary is always changing). I have been through denial. My head still believed that my body could do all that it could before. I still have my moments of denial. Unfortunately, what suffers most in this stage is my accountability. I want to be able to do all that I want to do for the world in the time frame my mind thinks I can do it. It just is not possible, and I have to learn to say no to myself.

I have to forgive myself for not being able to do all that I want to do. A symptom of my disease is ADHD. I have to reel myself in from having too many things going at once. I can tell when I am doing this, as my husband's eyeballs start spinning around in his head as he follows me. I can make him dizzy when I am in this mode. I have to listen when he yells, " Stop! Please stop!" I also have to be humble enough to ask for forgiveness from others for not living up to what I said I could do. This does not go over big at work. I am self-employed and my boss is not always so forgiving. I have come to a point where I see I need to choose clients that are willing to work with my disability in order to have the benefit of my expertise.

I grieve the loss of my prior self. It feels at times that I am getting old fast. I have learned to shed the "keeping up appearances". It is very hard to always be "looking good". This is when the world is falling down and you are looking like Donna Reed or a Stepford Wife. (I am dating myself here!) My sister use to hide her need for a cane. Now, if her body is feeling that way, she just uses it. In my life, I may be in wrinkled clothes and my house is not always picked up and perfect. I also fall behind in the mounds of paperwork that flood our personal life and work. I cannot do the number of hours at work that are demanded to be listed in society as a successful business, or to do all that I must to measure up to all the "shoulds" society puts out there as a parent and spouse. Energy and time is a commodity. I have a limited amount of energy and just so much time in a day that I have to offer. Therefore, I have to divvy them up to those I find most valuable in life:

1. **Family** – Ours, extended, and family members of choice

2. **Work** – It is my creative outlet.

3. **Volunteering** – I feel God has handed me these lemons to give the world some lemonade – one lemon at a time.

4. **My animals** – Two dogs and two fish

My family schedules life events around our ever-changing health status, sometimes up and sometimes down. I hope that I can instill in my daughter that she is not flawed. We just have a "thing" to deal with, as all people have their "things" to deal with. It does not change who we are, and it does not mean that we are any less important with what we can offer the world. There are so many out there who suffer. By sharing ourselves (in whatever way), we can send validation and caring out there that helps others to keep putting one foot in front of the other and making it through to the other side.

When my 8-year-old daughter was in the treatment rooms, she brought hope. Kids do one thing, and then they are on to the next. She may tell the story over and over about getting her pic line in, or when they pulled it, or when they drew blood each week to check her levels. Kids don't dwell in one place too long. Those experiences are just that, stories she shares. They are not reasons to stop doing. We would have the treatment, get something to eat, and if she had energy, go play a round of miniature golf before the next treatment. When we came home to New Jersey, she went right back to playing with her friends. She was a little different with what she could do, but we just did things differently. It was a great lesson for me to watch. Do what you have to do, and then go back to playing, because laughter is the best medicine.

For those that are going through chronic illness, either with someone you love or yourself, I offer the following to help you through:

1. **Life is a journey.** Sometimes we are climbing up the hill; sometimes we are coasting down. It just changes all the time. Work on going with the flow. Do the best that you can to accept your circumstances and make the best of the situation. I know when my mother-in-law lost all her hair to chemo we made her a lot of fun baseball caps to wear for all occasions. It was a small gesture, but I can tell you it made a sad time fun. It you are waiting for it all to get better to enjoy, then you may never get to enjoy anything for a long time, or ever. I know this sounds cliché, but life is short. Focus on the gifts, not the burdens.

2. **Set your priorities.** If you only have so much energy and time to share, be selfish and spend it doing what gives you the most pleasure.

3. **Having a chronic disease is a life transition.** Allow yourself time to go through all of the stages of denial, grief, and hopefully come to acceptance. Be willing to share with others so you can work through it. It is a gift you can give yourself. I think the reason kids go through it so well is because they do not know any better. They have less experience to compare it to. As adults, I see that we get stuck in the use-ta's. **Find a way for your past experiences to be a tool for the future, not a weight.**

4. **Give yourself a break to accept yourself however you are.** We all have something to offer, and we can learn from anyone if we keep ourselves open. Be patient and look for the gifts in yourself and others. Forgive yourself for not living up to what you want yourself to be able to do.

5. **Educate yourself on your disease or condition.** Be your own advocate. No one is more interested in your health than you (or possibly your parent). There is so much information out there on the Internet that is available. One of the things I have observed is that once the body becomes weakened with one issue, then it allows other problems to take hold. This is similar to our case and my sister's case. We have our main problem, and then our co-infections that complicate the problems. When the doctors treat only the symptoms, you run from one to another, addressing only the apparent issues. After awhile, you can start to feel as if you are just a hypochondriac. Find a doctor that will stop and take the time to look at the big combined picture. Don't let the others get you down. Keep putting one foot in front of the other, whether that is physically or emotionally.

The spirit in us all is a very powerful gift. It is a gift that can only be lost when we choose to give it up. Hold on to it. It is a gift that can change your world.

Notes:

_____

_____

_____

_____

_____

_____

_____

_____

_____

_____

_____

_____

_____

_____

_____

_____

_____

_____

_____

_____

_____

ABOUT THE AUTHOR

MARCELLA BERRY

Marcella Berry is President and CEO of Millionaire Mamaz, Inc., an exclusive organization for women, married, single, divorced or widowed who aspire to master the game of wealth. The organization introduces principles of balance and wealth in all areas of life to empower women emotional, physically spiritually, relationally and financially.

An expert on women's issues and nurse, Ms. Berry has a true passion for helping people. Ms. Berry was nominated woman of the year for Big Brothers and Big Sisters and she is a member of the International Advisory Board for the Professional Woman Network. As a Success and life coach. Ms. Berry has conducted training in the areas of Women's Issues and Diversity, Teen Image and Social Etiquette as well as Women's Wellness.

Ms. Berry also founded Successful Single Moms, a non-profit organization that provides information and resources to single moms globally. Ms. Berry is available as a keynote speaker and trainer on a national and international basis.

Contact
Marcella Berry
13547 Ventura Blvd. Suite #227
Sherman Oaks, Ca. 91423
(818) 474-7945
www.millionairemamaz.com
www.successfulsinglemomsglobalnetwork.com
Email: millionairemamaz@yahoo.com

THIRTEEN

SPORTING A NEW ATTITUDE

By Marcella Berry

Over the years, I have attended countless seminars, listened to hours and hours of tapes, read hundreds of books, and interviewed numerous successful people on the subject of personal development. I have discovered that learning, reading, and taping into a positive attitude is the very key to all self-help processes. The fact is, the most valuable asset you can posses is a positive attitude toward your life. Your attitude today determines your success tomorrow. The American Heritage Dictionary defines attitude as a state of mind or feeling with regard to some matter. The attitude you carry around makes an incredible difference in your life. My belief is, your attitude is you, and you are your attitude. The attitude you carry around makes an incredible difference in your life. Attitude determines whether you are on your way or in your way.

Attitude is Built From the Inside Out.

To discover true happiness, it's best to look within yourself, rather than depend on others or the world around you. The sad but true fact is that it is difficult to be happy if you depend on outside sources to bring you happiness. We all want to be happy and live fulfilled lives. Often, though, we demand too much of life. We set impossible criteria for what will make us happy. When those criteria are not met, we develop attitudes that only make matters worse. The very basic and most revealing question you can ask yourself is, "What does it take to make me happy?"

- Does that mean you have to be happy every minute of every day?

- Does every aspect of your work/job have to be fulfilling all the time?

- Does everyone have to do what you want them to do?

- Do you have to have more power than everyone else?

- Do you have to have more money than everyone else?

- Do you need to be recognized and rewarded for everything you do?

- Do you have to be loved by everyone you know?

Would you like to know how to bring more happiness in your life? I mean really bring happiness. No more anxiety, fear, jealousy, anger, irritation, resentment, boredom, unhappiness...you don't think that that kind of life is possible, do you? You think this way because no instructions came with this gift of life. Your life is a gift. A stereo comes with an instruction book; a car comes with an operator's manual. Hold on, and fasten your seat belt. I am getting ready to take you on a ride down a pathway to teach you how to sport a new attitude, and the have more happiness than you ever thought could be possible.

The first step in learning how to do this is to realize that the ways you use now to try and improve your life will always keep you bouncing like a yo-yo between happiness and unhappiness. If you are not continuously happy 100% of the time, it simply means that you are stumbling through life and not taking full advantage of the potential that has been placed in your head since the day you were born. Do you even know one person? Who is continuously happy? If you do, that person is using their higher consciousness.

People who continuously use their higher consciousness NEVER experience the disappointment of unfulfilled expectations. I know you try hard to have a good attitude about what life throws your way. So what's wrong? Most people who are unhappy don't know why they are unhappy. If they knew why unhappiness happens, they would at some point start correcting the situation so that they would be happy. The cause of unhappiness is not a mystery. It is actually quite simple. I know I have your attention, since you have read this far. I am now going to begin to share with you the attitude that will allow you to be happy 100% of the time. Even in situations that used to make you miserable (shortage of money, sickness, lost love, uncaring people etc....), are you ready? It will sound so simple that you might dismiss it all too quickly without really understanding how it applies to the very special conditions of your life in particular. But, doing it is not so simple. We all know the saying that it is easier said than done. You will need to be a strong woman.

Here it is... You automatically trigger feelings of unhappiness when people and situations around you do not fit in to your expectations. In other words, let's put it plainly, **expectations** create your unhappiness. It is your emotion-backed demands that make you suffer. It's not the world, the people around you, or even yourself! So, at this point, take a moment to forgive yourself. Whew! You cannot blame yourself for something you didn't know. Let's call these **unrealistic expectations and demands addictions**. An addiction is defined as something conditioned into the mind or body which, when it is not satisfied, *automatically triggers* a negative emotion of anger, jealousy, fear, anxiety, resentment, etc. All emotion-backed demands are addictions. I believe that addictions are a major cause of unhappiness.

Are you going to let the world and the people around you to control your attitude? There is a quote by J. Martin Kohe that says, "The greatest power that a person possesses is the power to choose." The root of your happiness is your joy. Don't let anybody steal your joy.

Do you let your happiness depend totally on the outside world? The outside world can never make you unhappy. Only YOU can create your unhappiness. For example…you really don't have to upset yourself if someone criticizes you. There's no law that requires you to be afraid of anything and trigger an emotion of fear, inadequacy or of anger. You don't have to make yourself irritated if the people you are with don't do what they have promised. Up until this point, you have probably been spending your life trying to manipulate the outside world in order to be happy.

Well, has it worked? Are you happy 100% of the time? Have you ever been successful in controlling the world in such a way that it could not make you unhappy? Your ego says to you that other people are doing it to you. But guess what? Yeah, you are right, you're doing it to yourself. Looking at the science of happiness, you will discover that there is (a) the outside event and (b) your inside programming that determines your response to the outside event. In life, you win some, you lose some. When you lose often, you can generate lots of suffering in your life.

This is because you have not trained your mind (your computer) so that it will not automatically trigger fear, anger or unhappiness. When the people and things around you do not fit the elaborate programming you have stored in your head, perhaps no one has ever fully explained how you can use the exceptional human computer in your head to do the job properly. After all, every computer requires some operating skill to make the best use of all the wonderful things, which it can do. The society in which you were raised led you to believe that you could win consistently enough to live a happy life if you had, more money, more prestige, more knowledge, more stuff that you can buy in stores. You have really accumulated a lot of stuff, haven't you? So then, are you always happy? Always? Are you really in love with living life? Are you in love with the prospective of facing a new day? Each day can be an interesting adventure. So let's learn how to enjoy every new day.

You kept yourself on a merry-go-round trying to make it in life by getting people and situations to fit your inner programs of security, sensation and power, pride, prestige, ability to manipulate and control. The way in which you try to solve one problem in your life usually creates the next problem in your life.

If you're lonely, your rational mind might suggest that you need more money so that you can attract friends or a love into your life. You then switch to a better paying job! Only to find you have added business worries. So your business worries now keep you from relaxing and enjoying friends and having love in your life.

When you work hard at acquiring something to make you happy and then you get it, do you then worry about losing it or damaging it? Wouldn't you like another one? A bigger one? A better one? Do you really want to know how to get the world outside your head to harmonize with your inside world? It's so simple. Instead of wearing yourself out trying to change the people and situation in your life, just concentrate on changing your addiction, which are your demands and your expectations. This is the only way to consistently get the outside and the inside to harmonize together. When you free yourself of the demands and expectations, you can still prefer that something happens a certain way. But if it doesn't, you can still remain happy, because it is not a condition for your happiness. It never occurs to people that this simple solution is the only way to do it. Isn't it easier to change your programming than to change people and situations to continuously fit your programming, which are those patterns that create the demands and expectations? There is a quote by Oliver Wendell Holmes that states, "What lies behind us and what lies before us are tiny matters compared to what lies within us."

Ten Strategies for Programming a Positive Attitude For Change.

1. Tap Into the Power of Your Subconscious Mind.

    Take the opportunity to program your mind with a positive attitude about the ongoing change. Instead of hitting the snooze button on the clock and whining about the challenges presented by this ever changing life, get up out of bed and thank God for giving you another day to enjoy life. Take a few minutes to create a plan for the day, and a strategy for dealing with the challenges of the day ahead.

2. Take Time to Reflect.

   Visualize yourself clearing out all the negativity in your mind and pessimistic thoughts and replacing them with an optimistic attitude. When you look in the mirror, you see the person who can do the most to improve your life, change your attitude, elevate your standards, and overcome your limitations. While you're looking in the mirror, monitor your inner dialogues. Be alert to any negative inner thoughts or self-criticisms regarding the change you are dealing with and cancel it.

3. Keep Your Goals and Values in Mind.

   Well-defined goals keep you focused on your end result. When you focus on your goals, you get a sense of control over your life, your self-esteem increases, and you begin to sense that what happens around you does not effect what is within you.

4. Maintain Balance.

   It is important to maintain physical, mental and spiritual balance. Rest, regular exercise, and health eating habits are important, because handling an unplanned event or expected change can be challenging.

5. Avoid Learned Helplessness.

   If you don't act on life, it will act on you. If you don't have any goals or direction in life, it will direct you. If you don't decide where you are going, life will take you to a place you probably never wanted to be. You may not be able to stop an unwanted change from happening in your life, but you can program yourself to take positive actions that make the most of it. So don't be inactive, be proactive.

6. Embrace Change.

Accepting change can take time. Generally speaking, this is a gradual process. Ultimately, the only thing you can change is yourself, and sometimes that changes everything.

7. Convert Threats into Opportunities.

When a change seems threatening, change it into an opportunity. A former colleague of mine worked in a program that underwent a complete overhaul. People who had held comfortable jobs for years were given new levels of expectations. There was a lot of bitterness. Many fought it. She had a great job. The nature of the business constantly changed, as technology increased. She accepted a transfer to a more demanding, less enjoyable job, but she chose to see it as an opportunity to expand her experience and widen her knowledge base. Not to any surprise, she thrived in her field of expertise, while many of her former colleagues remained bitter and unhappy.

8. Turn Change into a Challenge.

Challenges and change teach you something about yourself. Challenges and change force you outside your comfort zone. Challenges and change help you to realize again what is most important to you. I hold this step dear to my heart after becoming a widow. I embraced that I am a strong woman of faith and I can do all things through Christ, Jesus who strengthens me. (Philippians

4:13). I then moved to another city almost 500 miles from where I was raised, not knowing a single person. I believe Martin Luther King Jr. said it the best, "The ultimate measure of a man is not where he stands in moments of comfort, but where he stands at times of challenge and controversy."

9. Crank up Your Positive Energy.

When I feel negative energy coming on, I react to it like the flu. I do all I can to build up a natural resistance to it. With the flu, I start to increase my intake of vitamins and food supplements, and increase my layers of clothing. In the case of negative change, I create positive affirmations that I repeat. I tap into my lists of quotations and Biblical scriptures on the positive power of change. Here are a few:

The joy of the Lord is my strength. — *Nehemiah 8:10*

The power of positive thinking is stronger in fighting disease than all of the technology of modern medicine.
—*Thomas W. Allen, Psychologist*

Why settle for so little in life when you can have so much, just by daring to be different in your thinking. —*Catherine Ponder*

Helen Steiner Rice writes:
The more you love, the more you'll find
That life is good and friends are kind.
For only what we give away
Enriches us from day to day.

So, when we give away ourselves to get free of ourselves in being helpful to the less fortunate, we receive in return at least two magnificent gifts: a deep inner joy and a brand new enthusiasm for life and for people.

10. Develop an A-Team.

Work on building and nurturing relationships, so that you'll be able to draw upon them in times of need. These are the people that truly care about you. Lean on them in difficult and challenging times, because they know you will be there for them, as well.

Exercise: My "A" Team

List below each person who is part of your nurturing and supportive "A" Team. This is a person who is there for you always:

1. _____

   _____

2. _____

   _____

3. _____

   _____

4. _____

   _____

I would like to leave you with some affirmations that will have you sporting a new attitude. Say these affirmations to yourself aloud:

- "I acknowledge that changes are an essential part of life, and I am focused on finding solutions."

- "I will do whatever it takes to master this change and to create balance in my life."

- "I will make the changes within myself that are necessary to handle changes which are going on around me."

- "I will celebrate in each small step of the change process, and I will practice gratitude for the blessings I receive."

> *You have stripped off the old self with its practices, and have clothed yourselves with a new self, which is being renewed in knowledge according to the image of the creator.*
> — *Colossians 3:9-10*

My goal in writing this chapter was to make a difference in your life so that, in turn, you will make the difference in the life of someone else. I believe you have greatness within you. Now is the time to let the rest of the world know. Continue to put into practice the new skill set you have learned, and you'll notice a positive change in yourself, and in the way that people perceive you. Enjoy sporting your new attitude!

ABOUT THE AUTHOR

DR. KAREN B. WASSERMAN

Dr. Karen B. Wasserman is a licensed Clinical Psychologist (Indiana and Ohio), a Registered Nurse (Missouri and Ohio), an experienced consultant, and Life Success Coach. Whether working with special populations such as adults abused as children, people with bariatric concerns or individuals with chronic illnesses, Dr. Wasserman's focus has been on teaching others to find personal empowerment, to feel good about themselves, and most importantly, how to maintain positive self-esteem! Her goal throughout her career has been to help others to be about the business of enjoying life and finding the joy around them.

Born and raised in the Midwest, Dr. Wasserman received her Doctor of Psychology (Psy.D.) degree from Wright State University, School of Professional Psychology in Dayton, Ohio. As an Air Force spouse, she has lived in Texas, Germany, and along the Gulf of Mexico. She is a founder, and co-owner for nine years, of Fairhaven Clinic, Inc., (Private Mental Health) in Biloxi, Mississippi. She and her spouse also owned and operated a small book and gift shop nearby. Besides enjoying visiting her two children and collecting antiques (especially McCoy Pottery), she is an avid gardener. With her husband and a very small cat, she now makes her home in Olde Worthington, a suburb of Columbus, Ohio. This is house number fifteen!

Contact
Dr. Karen Wasserman
696 Oxford St.
Columbus, OH 43085
(614) 296-3522
drkarenB@columbus.rr.com
www.protrain.net

FOURTEEN

SELF-CARE OR SEL-FISH?

By Dr. Karen Wasserman

What is the difference between the terms selfish and self-care, self-love, self-esteem, or self-actualization? We certainly ascribe negative connotations to the concept of being self-ish as ONLY thinking of yourself (at others' expense), not sharing, not thinking of others' needs unless you can use it to your advantage, and taking all the credit for an accomplishment that was actually a team effort. We have been cautioned and conditioned from childhood to learn to think of others as well as ourselves. In the Judeo-Christian tradition, we learn to give up our seat on the train for someone older or infirm or pregnant, to pass the rolls to others before we take one, not to eat the last piece of pie, and "to share nice."

The question is then, what is 'all right,' permitted, allowed, encouraged for me to do for myself? Don't cut in line; wait till she's finished; give your little brother some of your drink; don't hog the bathroom – do these phrases sound familiar? Something every little girl learns is that in the restroom (the Loo, the W.C), you *must* wait your turn. It matters not how much you need relief, there is a line and there must be *waiting* in line. Turns are to be taken in order. We practice waiting in line, queuing up, not pushing or shoving, or being a 'line jumper.' How then does one learn to take care of the self? Is it even allowed to do so? I mean, all those others have needs too, right? So, is it ever OK to put myself first?

Some other phrases you might have heard applied as you grew up:

You are getting too big for your britches!	Pride goeth before a fall.
Don't get so puffed up about it!	Somebody needs to prick your balloon!

So, I remained confused about how to care for myself in the emotional sense. Everyone says they want me to have a sound feeling of self-esteem, yet no one ever defines what is a reasonable amount of self-care for self-worth? We have all been cautioned not to overdo it, but there seems to be scant instructions on what is appropriate and satisfying! Maybe you feel you are running your fingers along all the walls in order not to become lost. What/where are the directions for this part? I have a better idea of what not to do, and maybe little awareness of what is rational, logical, or can be acceptable for emotional self-care.

For instance, we speak of being assertive as being aware of our boundaries and simply standing up for ourselves; being forthright and not being passive or aggressive; not apologizing for being ourselves. When many women first learn assertiveness, they feel fearful and overwhelmed. If I have little experience in assertiveness or "I" statements, I am bound to feel uncomfortable when I am trying to practice saying something assertive or being assertive. Being uncomfortable though, is not the same thing as being wrong! Being assertive is an important step toward self-care. Some of us have found, on our way to being assertive, that we have spent a good bit of time being either passive, or even aggressive. The assertive person says, "Hi. Thank you for asking me to come over tonight, but I have something else planned." The passive person might say, "I'm sorry (immediately personalizing any guilt), but you know, I have to sew those letters on little Jack's jersey and I'm still doing the wash." Do you see how this person feels the need to excuse or explain all pertinent factors? The aggressive response might be yelling into the phone, "No, I have things to do, and I'm not coming over–that's that!"

For individual self-care, I recognize I have the right to say 'no', to be myself, and that I do not need to provide an explanation of my boundaries. As women, we are frequently of the notion that we must explain ourselves, as though to obtain the other person's agreement that, yes, that is an important reason for me not to change my mind/ plans about these events. In assertive terms, and logically, I do not need anyone's permission to set a particular boundary, or to choose one event over another. I know my reasons! It will not be awful or catastrophic if the other person does not love or approve of my decision. While it may increase my tension level initially, (to stand my ground – to define my limits), I am my own person, and I have the 'say so' as to priorities and choices. Screech! Halt! Did I really say that?

But wait, you may interject. What about not disappointing my relatives/my in-laws/my church group? Isn't that the consideration I am expected to show? Or, I really do not care that "X" knows what else I have to do, so why not just tell them about it? Reasonably, these are choices I might make, or might make on a different day. But, to feel that I am letting someone down because I do not always do what they what me to do, or to have the conviction that I must explain myself and all the details that went into my reasoned decision (or feel guilty because I do not explain), these ideas/convictions/feelings can mean I am not taking action of my own free will and of my own choice, but because of the social pressures and expectations that have been brought to bear on me. Or, at least I think these pressures are present. Perhaps I am still trying to please everyone, at the price of making my own choice, providing my own self-care, regardless of my happiness? Perhaps I am trying to circumvent guilt that might overtake me for putting my own needs/wants first? This is a choice I can make – but the difficulty lies within the reasons of my response and the response of others. If I acquiesce to the request, am I giving up a part of who I am and saying, therefore, that part of me is less important that the wishes of another? In fact, maybe I am just teaching others how to take advantage of me?

One person has some physical difficulties with her legs, with standing and lifting. It takes all her energy to do her job. A co-worker routinely asks her to do his copying, bring him items, and to provide him transportation. As a fully functional adult, he is capable of working the copier, retrieving items, and it is his own responsibility to provide transportation for himself. This is only logical and what is expected of any worker. The woman did not recognize she was being passive *and* teaching him to expect her to continue to do these things for him. She did not realize she was still trying to be the 'good' friend/mother/sister, until she was off work for a month, and the co-worker managed without her very well. When she returned, he again began to make demands on her time and energy! When she told him, assertively, that she was doing her own work, and reminded him he *was* able to do these things alone, he became irate and labeled her inconsiderate. This is where the principles of free will, self-care, and one's own choices takes center stage. Am I doing something because someone else wants me to AND I want to/am willing to do it? Or am I doing it because I'm convinced they will be angry with me if I stand my ground and make a different choice? **Brainstorm** now about requests made of you and what your feelings were when:

- A grandparent asked me to give them a ride to the store when my term paper was due.

- Friends asked me to help them move, and I planned to go to the lake that day.

- The boss asked me to get the packages ready to mail, but everyone is at the office, too.

- A friend asks me to come over and help paint (when he has 3 roommates who could help).

_____

_____

_____

_____

Did you struggle with feeling self-centered or selfish because you may have had other plans or commitments, especially to yourself, such that you wrestled with choices?

On one hand, we are told we need to care for our bodies, our minds, and our spirits. On the other hand, the not-so-subtle message is that everything else seems to have a greater priority than ourselves. How many times have you heard that it is important to exercise, eat properly, drink plenty of fluids, and sleep restfully? That it is important to take this or that supplement or avoid this/that additive? Magazine articles and books abound with such suggestions! How often do these tomes suggest you can set your boundaries so that to do good things for yourself, and take the time to do these things, is accepted *by you* as a priority, reasonable/proper, and the appropriate amount of self-care to have? Is it any less 'self-careful' to feel positively about yourself, as well? Will you have a 'swelled head' and be unable to fit through the door if you take time for yourself to read, sit on the deck, smell the flowers, listen to music, or daydream? Are these not just as reasonable and appropriate for our needs as exercise, grocery shopping, or dental check-ups? Are these not as important as that magazine's list of "15 Things to Do in 5 Minutes?" Is it horrible or wasteful to have 5 minutes for self?

We need a certain amount of self-esteem and valuation of self to make sound and positive choices on our behalf. Self-esteem indicates that I think well of myself and I am no worse, perhaps not better, but no worse, than any other individual. We are all human and have human limitations that include the options of making poor or unsound choices, making mistakes, or having skeletons in the closet. No, no, no, you may think- I am working as diligently as I possibly can to be perfect and informed (so I can *always* make the correct choices), and love my fellow humans, and avoid petty feelings of jealousy/envy! I do NOT get angry, or if I do, I certainly do not show it, and there are only skeletons in other people's closets. You can come look at mine anytime! Well, well, well, a candidate for sainthood, perhaps? But no, you say, I have my failings. I just don't let them get in the way of my successful perfection.

After all, can I have good self-esteem and still make all these human mistakes? We often pay lip-service to this idea, and yet have a shame attack if we do not live up to our own impossible standards. What if we can feel good about ourselves right now, as we are, on the way to becoming the person we want to be? Now, we did say person, not saint or angel-in-disguise. So, how does self-care fit into saintly ideas that I will not ever be too tired, too irritable, too harried, too scattered, too confused to do/say the right, correct and helpful 'thing' for another individual?

If we put self-care into our Valise of Valued Variables, we can better define when we need to take some time for self-care, and learn (Yes, we can STILL learn.) ways to provide this care to ourselves. No one else can know your needs as well as you, but this does require you to listen to your body, as well as the critical 'driver' of your mind. This difficulty in 'listening' to your body, or being IN your body, is one of our many obstacles to self-care. Are you sighing? Many sighs can indicate you are stressed and/or feel the need to keep emotions in check. The very first way most of us learned to stop our crying was by holding our breath. We recognize that there are muscles in the respiratory tract that can tense up, and with stress we do tense up all over. Thus, we can use the sighing as feedback to ourselves. "Whoa there, little filly. You need to slow down or release some stress here. Things are piling up!" Slowing down, listening to our body, helps us overcome the obstacle of inattentiveness (or disregard) to self.

Or, maybe you feel butterflies in your stomach, or even knots or pain in the midline of your chest or abdomen. Perhaps your 'gut' or your 'second brain' as we are coming to know it, is trying to tell you something about your stress level! Maybe you feel the stress in your neck, shoulders or hands? Do you recognize headaches, stiffening muscles, aches, or burning between the shoulder blades as indicators of stress? How about dry mouth, or frequent bathroom urges? **Identify** some of your personal body stress signals:

_____

_____

_____

_____

What did you learn? This feedback between body and mind may come naturally to some, but to the rest of us it represents work! Now, naturally, after I identify some of my stress indicators, I want to figure out what I can do to alter these responses, to change them, or to better recognize my obstacles. I can benefit from learning how to reduce my overall stress level, and know that I am making positive changes for myself that will help me to decrease the intensity or the frequency with which I feel stress. (And therefore, to the strength of my responses to stress.) This is reasonable self-care!

Stress is a fact of life, a tangible obstacle to self-care, and our bodies cannot discriminate emotional stress from a grizzly bear attack, or being chased by a giant squid. It is a matter of utmost importance in practicing self-care that I be familiar with my own responses to stress. Perhaps I am an individual who waits until I feel there is an elephant sitting on my chest before I can admit I am stressed. Or maybe I am dragging around as the last one in the office every night, not because I have so much more work to do than others, but because I am in 'burnout' and am taking so long to do my work. Maybe I find myself doing six things at a time and not finishing them, while I feel a tightness in my throat and difficulty swallowing or catching my breath. Certainly we have known others who sought out emergency services thinking their symptoms indicated a heart attack, only to determine the culprit was very powerful stress! We are only in this one body and stress really has no place to go unless we provide an outlet. Giving myself permission to recognize stress and allowing myself time to deal with it are two additional self-care strategies I truly need. Remember, it always takes longer than we think it is going to because we can think faster than we can 'do', and we are often overly optimistic and in a hurry to feel better.

List 5 situations in which you feel calm or at peace:

1. _____

2. _____

3. _____

4. _____

5. _____

What do you know about relaxation and when do you practice it? (No, watching TV does not count, as it has been demonstrated that those who watch the most TV are the most fearful.) Perhaps you are noticing the word 'practice' along with relaxation? Yes, we do need practice. We spend far more time in our lives being stressed (stand up straight; hold that tummy in; shoulders back) and not enough learning how to relax, much less practicing relaxation. We have a wonderful era that now provides specialized music, and fabulous scents to delight us. We can have marvelous plush covers to use, or mats to rest upon, and comfy clothes, just to relax. But, now that you are beginning to allow yourself to learn this type of self-care, what will you use, and when? Too many times we think, "Oh, I am feeling fine now, and I do not need to practice that. I'll do it some other time." Relaxation though, needs to be practiced regularly or the body-mind forgets how to do it, and it loses some effectiveness. If we need to practice our golf, piano, or swimming, we also need to practice our relaxation, or it will not be available when we most need to use it!

Identify what is soothing to you, whether it is smell, like watching fire or candles (yes these can have wonderful aromas), touching soothing fabrics like velvet, plush, satin, or dog/cat fur, or being touched, as in a massage, taking a long soak in a tub of bubbles *with candles* lighting the room, listening to special music or creating it, drawing, painting, digging, weeding, ice climbing, hang gliding or dancing, moving in planned ways with yoga or creative dance. Perhaps you have considered some recorded relaxation exercises, beginning with deep breathing, progressive muscle relaxation, visualization/imagery or sensory perception focusing? Perhaps you have considered Tai Chi or martial arts for self-care?

Your self-care dictum may include re-organizing your space at home, work, or both. Perhaps re-ordering your day, or giving yourself a day with a friend and taking turns learning about glaciers or foot massage or speaking another language, might be relaxing. Someone else can give you permission, but the biggest leap is to give *yourself* permission to do what you know is right for you. This is central to self-care. You are the only inhabitant of body-SELF, and the only one who can determine which types of relaxation work for you. So you try having a facial or a massage and think it is really icky and boring – what have you lost? Perhaps an hour, but now you also know what does not work for you, and that is information you did not previously have! You have also benefited from giving yourself permission to try new things and to determine whether they work toward the ultimate goal of overcoming your obstacles to self-care or not. Releasing yourself from the tyranny of 'having to know all the answers already' can provide a good bit of freedom, and releases some of the perfectionistic tendencies of wanting to 'get it right', especially getting it right the first time!

What is left to do is explore your inner world and determine what delights you, calms you, reassures you, comforts you, and re-energizes you for another day. Remember, you are the expert on yourself. Take the time to become acquainted with your inner self, inviting yourself to provide self-care, and allowing yourself to choose making YOU a priority! Your investment in self will be richly rewarded, and others who see how comfortable you are in your own skin can learn much from your example of how to provide self-care too!

"For fast acting relief, try slowing down." — Lily Tomlin

Recommended Reading

The Relaxation Response by Herbert Benson, Quill Books, New York, NY, 2000.

Inner Peace for Busy People by Joan Borysenko, Hay House, Inc., Carlsbad, CA, 2001.

Braiker, Harriet, *The Disease to Please* by Harriet Braiker, McGraw-Hill, New York, NY, 2001.

How to Raise Your Self-Esteem by Nathaniel Braden, Bantam Books, New York, NY, 1988.

Honoring the Self by Nathaniel Branden, Bantam Books, New York, NY, 1985.

I Know I 'm in There Somewhere by Helene Brenner, Gotham Books, New York, NY (Penguin Books), 2004.

Where the Girls Are by Susan Douglas, Three Rivers Press, New York, NY, 1995.

For Her Own Good by Barbara Ehrenreich & Deidre English, Anchor Books, New York, NY, 2005.

The Woman Who Broke All the Rules by Susan Evans & Joan Avis, Sourcebooks, Inc., Naperville, IL, 1999.

Silencing the Self by Dana Jack, Harper Perennial Publishers, New York, NY, 1993.

Can't Buy My Love by Jean Kilbourne, Simon & Schuster, New York, NY, 1999.

I Am A Woman Finding My Voice by Janet Quinn, Eagle Brook Publishers, New York, NY, 1999.

Wear More Cashmere by Jennifer Sander, MJF Books, New York, NY, 2005.

Notes:

ABOUT THE AUTHOR

JUDY HARRIS

Judy Harris has been working in Human Resources for over 20 years. She has worked for Rohm and Haas Company and the Albert Einstein Healthcare Network, and is presently the Human Resources Director for Frankford Candy & Chocolate Co. Her HR duties focus on recruiting, employee relations, organizational development, labor relations, and a host of other HR-related areas. She is also a trainer and consultant specializing in business communications, professional training, teambuilding, employee empowerment, and conflict resolution.

Judy facilitates seminars and workshops on self-esteem and empowerment. When Judy is not consulting or coaching, she is an adjunct professor at the University of Phoenix, where she teaches everything from HR Management to HR Law. She also hosts "It's Your J.O.B." (Jobs, Opportunities & Business) on WURD900am on Friday nights.

Judy is very active with these non-profits: Philadelphia Forward (a city government organization), The Delaware Valley Chapter of The National Alzheimers' Assn., Stand-up for Kids, the MS Society, Frankford-Northeast Rotary Club, and PhilAbundance.

Judy Harris holds a Master's Degree in Human Resources Management from Widener University and a Bachelor's Degree in Industrial Psychology from LaSalle University. She is a Certified Coach and has certification in E-Commerce, Women's Issues, and Diversity. She is available for workshops, seminars and motivational speaking on a local, national and international basis.

Contact
Harris Training & Development
(215) 276-1010
www.harristad.com

FIFTEEN

EMBRACING ALL STAGES OF LIFE

By Judy Harris

When we think about our past and envision the future, it is impossible to do so without reflecting on various stages that we have experienced and that we will experience. Just the thought of embracing, putting your arms around something, is an excellent way of thinking about stages of life. As you approach the stages, you should get a minimum of a Bachelor's Degree, whether you plan to be self-employed or work for someone else. If you are not self-employed, most companies offer some type of tuition-assistance plan that you can use. Remember: If you learn more, you will earn more. The key word: **EDUCATION.**

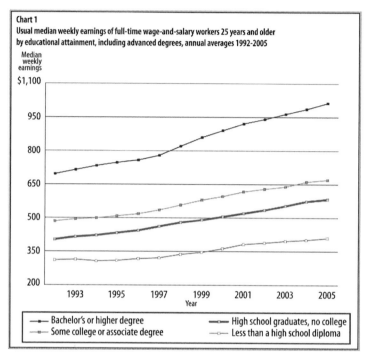

Chart 1
Usual median weekly earnings of full-time wage-and-salary workers 25 years and older by educational attainment, including advanced degrees, annual averages 1992-2005

As we mature and age, stages of life for adults will move in several directions. It is inevitable that we will go through various phases, and those phases will have their highs and lows. How we move about is paramount to our success.

When we talk about 'Stages of Life,' all of us have experienced **DEPRESSION** at one time or another. However, on occasion, feelings of depression can have a negative affect on our health and/or social lives. Walk these steps to cope with depression and ask yourself if you:

Set goals that are realistic. ⭕Yes ⭕No	
Focus on your positive experiences. ⭕Yes ⭕No	
Have a hobby and get socially active. ⭕Yes ⭕No	

Exercise as often as I can – daily if possible. ○Yes ○No
Keep a list of your positive accomplishments. ○Yes ○No
Express anger in an assertive manner. ○Yes ○No
Know what your strengths are and try to develop them. ○Yes ○No
Do some volunteer work, preferably with a non-profit organization. ○Yes ○No
Know the cause of depression and try to be positive about the future. ○Yes ○No

Preparing Yourself—As we progress through various stages of life, it is important to take care of yourself, network, and have attainable goals. Ask yourself these questions:

	Yes	No	I Will Do This On/By
Do you have an up-to-date resume?			
Are you a member of a professional organization?			
Have you decided where you want to be professionally in 5 years?			
Do you subscribe to a professional organization magazine?			
Have you taken a vacation within the past two years?			

Have you let your family know your goals?			
Are you comfortable navigating the Internet?			
Are you assertive?			
Are you ready to move to a higher level in your career?			
Do you have a mentor or coach?			
Do you have realistic goals?			
Do you take a daily multi-vitamin?			
If applicable, are you practicing safe sex?			
Have you had your yearly mammogram?			
Do you have faith in and pray to a divine being?			
Do you exercise regularly?			

If it has not already happened to you, it will – **MENOPAUSE**! It is a natural event that normally occurs between the ages of 50 and 53.

Hot Flashes	Loss of Sexual Desire	Night Sweats	Dry Skin	Depressed
Weight Gain	**SYMPTOMS OF MENOPAUSE**			Breast Pain
Hair Loss				Mood Swings
Tiredness	**Check those you have experienced**			Anxiety
Headaches	Cravings for Sweets	Trouble Sleeping	PMS	Mood Swings

There are natural and holistic ways you can reduce or eliminate some of the symptoms that happen during menopause.

- DO NOT smoke -- cigarettes can cause early menopause.

- Exercise often to strengthen your bones.

- Take calcium and vitamin D.

- Eat a low-fat diet.

- Control your blood pressure, cholesterol, and other risk factors for heart disease.

- Avoid caffeine, alcohol, and spicy foods.

- Eat foods that contain soy, and take a daily dose of black cohosh (but don't take them if you have estrogen-dependent cancers).

You may fall into one of these stages: Married, living together unmarried, dating, or in a committed relationship. In 2007, more than half of the couples in the U.S.A. live together unmarried.

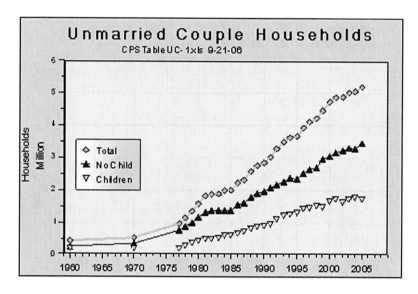

Divorce

Let's face it – it may or may have happened to you. The bottom graph is the divorce rate; the TOP graph is the marriage rate. Current as of Nov. 23, 2006 and reprinted from the Bureau of Labor Statistics, and the information is 'public domain.'

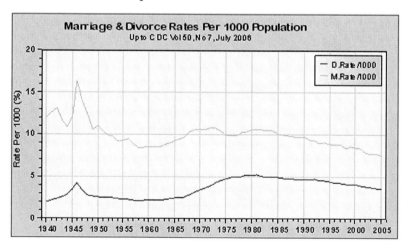

True/False Quiz (answers after the chart below):

☐True ☐False – The ratio of marriages to divorces is 2 to 1.

☐True ☐False – In 1998, TOTAL marriages showed a sharp drop.

☐True ☐False – Marital Status for FEMALES 15 and over (1950-2005) shows that the population of unmarried women will soon surpass the number of married women.

☐ True ☐ False – The number of UNMARRIED COUPLE HOUSEHOLDS (couples living together) is increasing steadily.

☐True ☐False – Children living with only one parent has increased from 9% in 1960 to 30% in 2005.

Answers: All are TRUE

Relationships

Which one of these categories best describes you? Follow the advice that goes along with each category.

☐ I am Married.

- Pray together to stay together.

- Be honest and be faithful.

- Don't fight over money – you'll never have enough, anyway.

- Remember birthdays and anniversaries.

☐ I am Unmarried and living together.

- Put a time limit on how long the living together phase will last.

- Do not live with a partner if children are involved. Cohabitating parents break up at a higher rate than married parents; the effects are just as devastating as a divorce.

- Get engaged first.

- Think twice before you live together unmarried. — KEH.

☐ I am Divorced.

- Take care of your most important needs: financial, personal security, healthcare.

- Utilize all the support you can get (phone, email, etc.)

- Take good care of your children and yourself. Continue to heal.

- Learn to laugh again.

☐ I am Dating.

- Do your homework; know as much as possible about the person you are dating.

- If you are not in a celibate relationship, do not have unprotected sex. *

- Do not sleep with your date too early in the relationship.

- Demand respect.

* I want to emphasize the importance of using a male or female condom, because of the high incidences of HIV/Aids. Women of color are especially affected by HIV infection and AIDS.

These are alarming stats from: htttp://www.cdc.gov/hiv/topics/women/resources/factsheets/women.htm

| | Diagnosis of HIV/AIDS in females aged 15-39 years | | | |
| | 2001 | | 2005 | |
	No.	(%)	No.	(%)
White	1,218	(63)	996	(56)
African American	5,299	(62)	4,091	(58)
Hispanic	1,192	(60)	819	(57)
Asian/Pacific Islander	31	(55)	62	(66)
American Indian/ Alaska Native	23	(52)	39	(68)

Are you at the stage of becoming an **EMPTY NESTER**? If you have moved (or are moving) into the Empty Nest stage, consider it as an opportunity to take advantage of your newfound freedom. Rank below from 1 through 10, each item you will do with your newfound freedom.

Rank beow from 1 through 10: (1 = the most important up to 10 being the least important item you will do with your new found freedom.)

___ Invest the $$$ you will save on food, utilities, and clothing.

___ Travel more and take longer vacations.

___ Learn a new hobby.

___ Volunteer with a non-profit organization.

___ Spend more time with friends and family.

___ Become more involved in your church.

___ Join a social group of other empty nesters.

___ If you are married, rekindle the old flames.

___ Keep in contact with your child via email.

___ Consider furthering your education or get additional training.

Finally, we should always experience a stage of life when **IT'S ALL ABOUT YOU** and you may be contemplating stepping on stage and raising the curtain to owning your own business. These are my top 10 pieces of advice that entrepreneurs have given me:

Starting a Business Check List:

1. Have a take-charge attitude; be assertive, but not aggressive.

2. Start out with a business plan that will cover your overhead, expenses, office, etc.

3. Before starting, save as much money as you can.

4. Ensure that all contracts and agreements are in writing; oral contracts are hard to prove.

5. Start out small.

6. Your personal assets should be protected, so that a creditor can't go after them.

7. Know your competition.

8. Understand how – and if – you will make a profit.

9. Keep your credit in good standing by paying your bills and taxes on time.

10. Know who to contact and where to go for services needed.

You may be at a stage in your life where you're pondering going into business for yourself. Below is a "YES, NO, MAYBE SO" quiz to gauge your entrepreneurial possibilities.

	Yes	No	Maybe So
1. Are you a go-getter and don't give up until you succeed?			
2. Do you like making your own plans?			
3. Do you bounce right back up when you hit bottom?			

4. Do you see yourself achieving more each year?			
5. Do you expect to conquer your lifelong goals?			
6. Are you passionate about succeeding at your work?			
7. Do people come to you for advice?			
8. Do you look for a better way to accomplish a task, rather than complain?			
9. Are you comfortable thinking out of the box?			
10. Do you stick with a task until you succeed?			
11. When you make a mistake, do you view it as a learning experience?			

Key

Majority "Yes": Go for it – It's all about YOU.

Majority "No": You should do some soul searching before becoming self-employed.

Majority "Maybe So": Think about what you really want to do.

If you are nearing the stage of life when you want to become an entrepreneur, contact:

• The Professional Woman Network: (www.prowoman.net)

- National Association of Women Business Owners: (www.nawbow.org)

- SCORE - (www.score.org): Volunteer counselors give free advice to entrepreneurs.

- Women Impacting Public Policy: (www.wipp.org) Advocates on behalf of women.

- SBA/Office of Women's Business Ownership: (www.sba.gov/womeninbusiness)

- Women-21: (www.**women-21**.gov) Provides general information for women entrepreneurs.

Heath Care Challenges

One of the most challenging stages I've experienced was the care of my aunt who was diagnosed with Alzheimers. I found solace by volunteering with the Delaware Valley Chapter of the National Alzheimers Association. If you find yourself having to care for a relative with Alzheimers:

- Give them easy activities such as folding clothes.

- Involve them in conversations about their childhood.

- Take walks or go out for ice cream.

- Become involved in Alzheimers support groups, events, etc.

- If they do something that is funny – laugh and bring them in on what's so funny.

- When they ask the same question several times, only answer once and redirect their attention.

- Make notes about their memory and mood in a journal.

- Talk to them, and when possible, include them in cooking, cleaning, reading, simple crafts.

Regardless of what we decide to do, we are going to go through a stage of **Transition**, whether this includes continuing our education, deciding to divorce, starting a new business, or being faced with health challenges (or those of **others**). It is important to know your strengths and weaknesses. You should focus your energy and keep your eye on the prize. Most importantly, embrace each stage of life and prepare for the next. Continue with a positive attitude and know that change is **inevitable**, and often very positive.

I wish you a smooth journey as you transition through the stages of YOUR life.

Notes:

ABOUT THE AUTHOR

BRENDA MCDOWELL-HOLMES, MBA

Brenda McDowell-Holmes is Founder, President and Chief Executive Officer of McDowell-Holmes & Associates, Inc. The company was established in 2005 to provide personal and professional development services for youth, school districts, business professionals and organizations of all sizes.

McDowell-Holmes & Associates has successfully mentored and counseled youth to overcome obstacles to fulfilling their life purpose. Youth development sessions include Save Our Youth, Stress Management for Youth and Leadership Development. The company also conducts personal and professional development seminars on various topics, including marketing strategies for consultants, women's issues, diversity, wellness and branding and image projection.

Ms. McDowell-Holmes is a veteran of diversified experience in the corporate environment. She is certified in Diversity, Professional Speaking, Customer Service and Youth Issues. She holds a Masters Degree in Business Administration/Human Resources and a Bachelors Degree in Business Administration/Management. Ms. McDowell-Holmes is also a member of several professional organizations, such as Professional Woman Network (Advisory Board), American Business Women's Association, National Association for Female Executives and National Black MBA Association and Toastmasters International. She is also a Real Estate investor.

Ms. McDowell-Holmes is the co-author of several soon to be released books: *A Women's Guide for Overcoming Obstacles, Transition & Change, Women s Leaders: Strategies for Empowerment & Communication, and Beyond the Body: Developing Inner Beauty.*

She dedicated this book project to her wonderful father and beautiful mother and angel. She wishes to acknowledge her husband, Willie Holmes, her gomother, Carolyn Crawford, her sisters, brothers, nieces, nephews, and closest friends who believe in her.

"Thank you Daddy for believing in me; now I can help motivate people to change their lives."

Ms. McDowell-Holmes is available to conduct seminars and workshops on a local, national and international basis.

Contact
McDowell-Holmes & Associates, Inc.
P.O. Box 1583
Stockbridge, Ga. 30281
(404) 663-2418
brholmes@bellsouth.net
www.protrain.net

SIXTEEN

LIVING A MORE SPIRITUAL LIFE

By Brenda McDowell-Holmes

What is Spirituality?
According to the dictionary, spirituality has many definitions, some of which include:

- pertaining to or consisting of things that can't be seen

- relating to the soul, as opposed to one's physical nature

- something supernatural

- having a moral or religious nature

- having to do with sacred matters

- belonging to the church

As you can see, spirituality has a wide range of meanings. Perhaps that is why there is such a divergence of interpretations for what it means to be spiritual. For some people, spirituality is deeply rooted in their religion and cannot be easily separated, making the two words synonymous. For others, spirituality could simply be connecting with nature and the realization that there are universal powers greater than oneself that created things like mountains, trees, and rivers. For me, spirituality has meant getting closer to and having a relationship with a higher power, which I call "God." Understanding your own personal definition of what spirituality means to you will help you in your quest to attain a more spiritual life.

Journaling: Exercise 1

Take a few moments now to think about what spirituality means to you by writing down how you would answer the following questions:

1.   How would I define spirituality?

2.   Are my religious beliefs an integral part of my spirituality?

3.   Is there a particular place I can go to feel more spiritual?

4.   What are my spiritual beliefs?

5.   What is the relationship between my spirituality and the other parts of my being, like my emotional nature and my intelligent mind?

Only when you clearly understand your own personal beliefs about spirituality can you then determine if you need to live a more spiritual life.

Why Become More Spiritual?

One of the main reasons to become a more spiritual person is because it will give you a great feeling of peace.

"To win true peace, a man needs to feel himself directed, pardoned, and sustained by a supreme power, to feel himself in the right road, at the point where God would have him be – in order with God and the universe. This faith gives strength and calm."— Henri Frederic Amiel

So many people in the world today are uneasy and afraid. They feel helpless and hopeless about things like wars, natural disasters, and other things beyond their control. However, by getting in touch with their spiritual natures, people can understand that there is a Divine Plan that is greater than they are. So, while they may not understand why all these things are happening, they feel reassured that there is a greater purpose for everything that happens in life. Then, instead of feeling helpless, people can get in touch with the powerful nature of their spiritual selves, which gives them strength to endure whatever happens in life. People who are in-tune with their spirituality also tend to have a strong sense of purpose. They know who they are and what they want to do with their lives, enabling them to live more happy and fulfilled lives.

Journaling: Exercise 2
In order to determine your need to lead a more spiritual life, take some time to answer the following questions:

1. How would I rank the importance of spirituality in my life?

    _____ Top Priority

    _____ Very Important

    _____ Important

_____ Not Very Important

_____ Low Priority

2. How peaceful do I feel? Explain in depth why you believe you do or do not feel peaceful.

3. How empowered am I in my life?

4. Do I know the direction I want my life to take? Discuss this in detail.

5. Am I happy with my life?

Another reason to get in touch with your spirituality is that you will live a healthier and longer life. Spiritual people understand that their bodies are temples and treat them well by nourishing them with healthy food and plenty of exercise. On the other hand, people who have deficiencies in their spiritual lives often try to fill the void with other things, and many times these things turn into bad habits or addictions. Some of these include using illegal drugs, smoking or drinking too much, or overeating. Take a close look at your life. Do you have any bad habits or addictions that may be masking a void in your spiritual life? Make a list of them. Then come up with a game plan for overcoming these negative influences in your life. Perhaps you might consider getting counseling, or going to meetings where people with similar challenges are discussing how they are coping with their situations. By taking steps to eliminate your negative behaviors, you will gain purpose and be on your way to a healthier, more spiritual life.

Journaling: Exercise 3

Create a chart like the one below and list all the healthy and unhealthy things you do. Then examine whether you are taking good care of yourself and treating your body like the temple which houses your spiritual being.

Healthy Behaviors	Unhealthy Behaviors

Steps For Becoming More Spiritual

Once you have determined your need for becoming a more spiritual individual, you will need a game plan. So we are going to discuss the steps you can take to begin to live a more spiritual life.

Meditation/Prayer/Affirmation

One of the techniques you might find helpful in both having a more spiritual life and overcoming your negative patterns is through using meditation, prayer, and/or affirmations. Meditation is a way to empty your mind of all thoughts, allowing you to focus on nothingness, stillness, and silence. So often in our hustle and bustle world of computers, television, and cell phones, we don't have the chance to be quiet and focus on what's really important. As a result, we lose touch with our inner selves and our essential spiritual nature.

Meditation gives you an opportunity to come to know your invisible self. It allows you to empty yourself of the endless hyperactivity of your mind, and to attain calmness. It teaches you to be peaceful, to remove stress, to receive answers where confusion previously reigned. — Dr. Wayne Dyer

Some people meditate by using C.D.'s with music, while others chant a sound or phrase over and over, while still others sit quietly and focus on a peaceful scene or even on just the blankness. Use whatever technique works best for you and allows you to calm your mind. Your goal is to block out all the things that usually clutter your mind: work, bills, appointments, etc. and to get in touch with your calm, peaceful, spiritual self.

Prayer is another technique that is widely used by people in a variety of faiths. Through prayer, people are able communicate with a Higher Power, which allows them to express their worries and concerns. By doing so, they are able to release these problems and have faith that they will be solved. Many people find that praying on a regular basis allows them to worry less and feel less stress because they have confidence that their Higher Power will guide them in the right direction. People also use prayer to express their feelings of gratitude for all the blessings in their lives. By doing so, they are showing appreciation for all of the goodness they experience. When people are grateful, they are more likely to be happy, because they realize all the reasons why their life is a blessing.

Both meditation and prayer can benefit from using affirmations. These are simply positive statements people make about themselves and their lives that reveal the truth about who they are and what is happening in their world. Simple examples of affirmations include: "I am a successful, loving mother and wife." "I live a life full of happiness and love." "I am grateful for the blessings of a loving family, fulfilling work, and my excellent health." The reason positive affirmations are so important is that they counteract all the negativity we experience on a regular basis. How many times have other people told you that you couldn't do something? How many times have told yourself you weren't smart enough or talented enough to achieve what you wanted? It seems like the only news that is reported is bad news: murders, fires, deaths. So it's much easier to be in a negative mindset than a positive one. However, you need to remember that there is a great deal of power in your thoughts and words. If you believe you are unlucky and then say so, that is the reality you are affirming for yourself. You will find that you never win the lottery or get the promotion or whatever it is that your heart desires. On the other hand, if you say that you are a really lucky person and affirm this out loud, you will find that you seem to get a lot more breaks, and are much more likely to get what you want than someone who has a negative attitude. When you affirm good things in your life, then you call on a universal power greater than yourself to help you achieve all that you believe is possible for yourself. Words have power. So watch what you say. When you catch yourself saying things like "I can't . . ." or "I'm not . . ." try reframing what you say.

Journaling: Exercise 4
Write down the negative things you say or think in the course of one week in the left hand column, then write down positive statements you could replace them with in the right hand column.

Negative Thought or Statement	Positive Affirmation

Journaling: Exercise 5

Practice writing positive affirmation about yourself. Fill in the blank spaces with positive statements about who you are and what you want from life.

I am _____

My life is _____

My work is_____

My health is_____

I am grateful for_____

Repeat these affirmations daily in either your meditation or prayers, and you will find these statements are reflecting the truth of who you are and what your life is manifesting.

Fasting

Another technique you can use in order to lead a more spiritual life is to fast. Fasting involves going without food and drink for a certain period of time. Many religions advocate fasting as a way to help people strengthen their faith. Also, many great spiritual leaders have made a practice of fasting in order to help them focus on their spirituality. You may be wondering how being hungry or thirsty can help you be more spiritual. But the fact is that all too often people become focused on material things (like food) which prevent them from exploring more the deeper meaning of life. How many times have you celebrated a special occasion with a meal? Have you ever thought about other ways you could celebrate? Maybe you could dance or sing or just sit down and have a long talk, congratulating the person on his/her special occasion. Food is such a widely accepted way of socializing with others that we often use it as a crutch, which stifles other creative ideas of connecting with others. When you fast, it allows you to closely examine your relationship with what you eat to see if it is a healthy one. Are you using food to truly nourish your body, or are you using food as a distraction to keep you from dealing with your problems. Fasting allows you the extra time you would have spent preparing, eating, and then cleaning up after your meal to think about other things that are more important in your life. As a result, fasting can be an invaluable tool for living a more spiritual life.

The goal of fasting is inner unity. This means hearing but not with the ear; it is hearing with the spirit, with your whole being. The hearing that is only in the ears is one thing. The hearing of understanding is another. But the hearing of the spirit is not limited to the ear or to the mind. Hence, it demands the emptiness of the faculties. And when the faculties are empty, then your whole being listens. There is then a grasp of what is right before you that can never be heard with the ear or understood with the mind.
—Thomas Merton, "The Living Bread"

Fasting is a physical discipline and probably should not be undertaken for more than one day at a time. There are many different ways to fast. Research what is good for you and then try it to see if it helps you with your spiritual growth. When you decide to fast, the only person you should discuss it with is your doctor so you can make sure that you have no health issues that would make this a dangerous activity for you. Don't tell anyone else you are fasting because you want them to see what a spiritual person you are. Fasting is a private activity designed to help you focus on understanding yourself and your faith better by eliminating anything that might distract you, like food. In a way, fasting is the ultimate form of meditation and can only be done effectively in private. If, during the time you are fasting, you receive an invitation to dinner, simply politely decline by stating you are not available and try to schedule another time to have dinner.

Journaling: Exercise 6
Choose a day to fast when you can relax and spend some time meditating/praying. Write down your thoughts and feelings, especially anything that crosses your mind about food or drink. Take some time to analyze whether or not you have a healthy relationship with the things you eat and/or drink. The day after your fast, analyze whether or not you think this practice helped you spiritually and if you plan to make fasting a regular part of developing your inner self.

Giving

Yet another way to live a more spiritual life is to become a giver. Many religions advocate tithing 10% of your income to your church or another charity of your choice. The theory behind tithing is that you are giving back to the universe abundance you have been blessed to receive. Giving shows a thankful heart. When you give, you are also showing your belief that there is more than enough in the world to go around, and that you know that you will continue to be blessed with everything you need. When your hand is open to give, it is also open to receive; however, when you close your hand with a tight fist and refuse to share with others, you also have closed yourself off to being able to receive the blessings that might otherwise be available to you.

> *I have found that among its other benefits,*
> *giving liberates the soul of the giver.* — Maya Angelou

Giving isn't limited to money. Many people also give their time, which in today's world is a very precious commodity. When you volunteer your time to share your knowledge or help other people, you receive innumerable blessings. Sometimes these come in the form of close friendships, and sometimes they take the form of good feelings of generosity. When people are depressed, one of the best things they can do is help others. By doing so, they will often see that their own problems are small in comparison to what other people have to face. Giving is an important component of faith, which in turn, is the real key to all spirituality. You should plant a seed of giving to receive a harvest.

Journaling: Exercise 7
Over the course of the next month, write down the ways you give. Write down when you give your money or time to others. This would include things like giving tips, helping a person whose car battery is dead, etc. Then write down what spiritual benefit you gained from your act of giving. You might use the following chart as a guide:

Act of Giving	Spiritual Benefit

The Importance of Faith in Spirituality

If you want to lead a more spiritual life, you must have faith. Faith is the foundation of all spirituality. According to the Bible, *"Faith is the substance of things hoped for, the evidence of things not seen."* It is hard to believe in things you can't see, but it is crucial to living a more spiritual life. All the tools you use to become more spiritual including meditation, prayer, affirmations, fasting, and giving, are all acts of faith. Through meditation, prayer, and affirmations, you are expressing faith in a universal power to help you become the person you want to be, and to achieve your heart's desire. Fasting and giving both show your faith in an abundant universe, which allows you always to have enough to eat, as well as the other necessities of life. In fact, everything you do that has a spiritual component is based on your faith.

Daddy gave me a good example of faith, one which I want to share with you. He said, "Faith is like walking and feeling the wind blowing in your face. You do not see the wind blowing, but you feel it on your face." Faith is knowing that, even though you can not see something, you know it is there. We must always have faith in what we believe. That is the essence of our spirituality and the key to living a more spiritual life.

Notes:

ABOUT THE AUTHOR

PAMELA THOMPSON

Pamela Thompson received her Bachelor's of Science degree in Business Management from Spring Hill College and is currently working on her Masters degree. She has received several honors as a college student.

Her professional career has been in sales and consulting which has allowed her to travel throughout the United States. She is a licensed mortgage consultant and president of Thompson & Associates which provides advice regarding business start-up.

Pamela Thompson is a member of the Professional Woman Network and a certified Youth Trainer with additional certification in Women's Issues & Diversity.

She serves on the board of directors for YWCA where the goal is to eliminate racism and empower women. The YWCA supports homeless children and provide daycare and after-school care; it also has several programs to educate women to read and to learn computer technology. Pamela also volunteers her time at the Mobile County Public School System, as she believes that parent involvement is critical to the success of the children.

Pamela Thompson is the proud mother of four children Brent, Fernando, Alicya, and Christopher. She continues to lead by example while educating women and children of the availability of vast opportunities in our society.

Contact
Pamela Thompson
7844 Heaton Dr E
Theodore, AL 36582
(251) 402-0573
Pamela36582@peoplepc.com

SEVENTEEN

MANAGING LIFE STRESSORS

By Pamela Thompson

Managing life's stressors can be a challenge! Let's review the meaning of this title in its simplest form according to Webster's Dictionary. "Managing" is to be in charge of something; to achieve something with difficulty; cope in difficult situations; to survive or continue despite difficulties, to handle and control something. "Life" is defined as the time a person or thing is alive or exist. "Stress" is defined as a strain felt by someone mentally, emotionally, or physically caused by anxiety or overwork. A synonym of stress is" worry", which is defined as a troubled state of mind.

To begin, look at the positives in your life. Look at what is going *right* in your life. Sometimes you have to get to a place where everything is at a standstill; perhaps you need to have solitude so that you may focus on the gifts you have in life. Once you are in a calm state of mind and body, let your thoughts move to the stressors in your life. To become truly successful in managing life's stressors, you must first identify the stressor. Calmly analyze the factors that are causing you stress, and begin to consider solutions that will eliminate or "manage" these stressors. If you are running at a frantic pace, you will be unable to clearly see the BIG picture as to how the stressors may be managed. You must create a calm state of mind and find a peaceful environment before strategizing your stress management plan. Let us look closely at the stressors that are common to most women. They include: **family, career, time,** and money.

Family

We love our families, but they can be major pains in our lives. It does not have to be this way. Let's start with a spouse or significant other. First, set boundaries for them and explain what you will and will not tolerate.. Second, you must communicate (no one is a mind reader); let them know what is on your mind and how you feel. Finally, let it out this may sound silly, but it works. If you have built-up stress and anger, find a place of solitude and all by yourself **SCREAM.** (*I do, of course, suggest you practice this technique only at home alone or out in a remote area)* This technique is not to be used against your spouse or significant other but just as a stress-releaser for you). You may also consider writing a letter, but tearing it up, or pounding a pillow with your fist. You will be surprise how much better you feel.

Activity #1

Describe something that increases your stress level about your spouse or significant other.

How do you generally respond to this stressor?

_____

What can you do differently in regard to your reaction to this stressor?

_____

Another family stressor is our precious children. They raise our stress level from the time of conception until they leave this earth (especially the teenage years). Raising children seems difficult and complicated but the stress can be lessened if you are **proactive**. Rather than over-reacting to every behavior that your child displays, consider behavior boundaries; if they step over the line, there are consequences. But try to remember your life as a child. Consider how your parents raised you and what you would have done differently had you been the parent. The greatest gift you can provide your child is that of unconditional love. Another gift is taking care of yourself and having adequate stress outlets such as hobbies and time alone. Here are five keys to providing a stable home life for your children, which will in turn, lessen stress level for the whole family:

Love: Accept your child unconditionally; tell them every day that you love them; provide plenty of hugs and encouragement.

Security: Be a stable role model for your child; provide a loving, peaceful home life without drug or alcohol addiction; be there for your child always.

Understanding: Be empathetic with your child; be patient with them.

Discipline: Provide consistent discipline with consequences for poor behavior. Remember that beating, shoving or name-calling is not discipline, but abuse.

Prayer: Provide a spiritual life for your child. Be a role model in living a Godly life; incorporate prayer into your family life.

Finally, we have the extended families, uncles, aunts, cousins, in-laws and outlaws. These individuals can be **very** stressful. One of the greatest stress reducers for family problems is to either openly communicate the problem (calmly), be patient, remove yourself from the situation, or distance yourself emotionally. Of greatest importance learning to forgive. Take off the ball and chain of constantly carrying around anger and hurt. Forgive the perpetrator. Communicate your feelings and then get over it! We all know you feel much better when loving a person than hating a person. If feels better when you smile and laugh than frown and cry. If you have family members that are stressing you out please be honest with them. When you tell the truth there is nothing else to say because everything is out in the open. The truth will set you free and release much unnecessary stress. Now what the other person does with the information is totally up to them, but love and truth should take the stress level down a couple of notches! Have you told a family member how you really feel?

Career/Job

Another stressor in life would be your career or job. (Do you have a career or a job?). A career is something a person chooses to do and they put into it what they want out of it. A job on the other hand is something that a person *has to do in order to live.* My advice would be to do something you love! That's a heart-based career! Let's take a closer look at your working life.

Activity #2

What are you currently doing for work? Is it a job or a career?

_____

Are you stressed in this current position? Why or why not?

_____

What can you do to lower the stress levels?

_____

_____

_____

If your work is "just a job", what might you do to take the steps to prepare for the career of your dreams? What would that career be?

Please do something you enjoy in life because it is very short. However, be realistic, because *every* career has stressful times! I am a mortgage consultant and a born sales person. This career can be stressful 98% of the time, but it is all in the way that you approach your job or career. A sales person's work is never done. You always strive to do better daily. Whatever you did yesterday was yesterday! Sales people are forever looking to the future and challenging themselves. This in itself is stressful to many women; however, there are those who **thrive** under this stress. Be truly introspective and look into yourself as to what type of work you can really handle! Find the career of your dreams and build in stress outlets in your life that will serve as a buffer. Know what you can and cannot handle.

Money

Can you say stressor almighty? This thing called money can make women lose their minds You can either have too much or not enough. Some people may say you can never have too much money. I say you can! Money can ruin a person's life (squandering on impulse buying; increasing your debt; competing against others) and it also has the power to make a woman's life much more full as she uses and invests the money wisely; allowing the money to work *for* her. My reasoning behind too much is that you have more than enough money than you know what to do with i. You have purchased all the cars, homes, jewelry, and clothing and still not have a peace of mind. On the other hand, with no money you wish that you could buy a car, a house, one nice piece of jewelry, and stop spending more than 50% of your income on clothing to try and make yourself feel better. Why does money have this effect on people? What matters is that you are wise with your money and not allow it to cause you undue stress! Do what makes sense with your finances! Begin asking yourself if you spend money unwisely? Why are you spending this money? Is it for what you truly need, or are you simply desiring to WANT, WANT, WANT? Wise words from my Bishop Levy H. Knox, Pastor and Founder of Living Word Christian Center: *"You make the money, don't let the money make you."*

Activity #3

Describe your current financial status and situation:

List 3 ways in which you can change your current financial status

1. _____

2. _____

3. _____

Time

Time is a stressor we deal with everyday; it can be cruel, rude, and inconsiderate but always consistent. It does not care that you are not finished with your shopping at Christmas. It does not care if you are not prepared for the Thanksgiving holiday. Time does not say" I know you have a project due and I will wait for you." Nor does it say "I know you only had four hours of sleep so I will wait for you to rest before you have to go to work". Time does not say "I know you want to be 25 again so let me roll back the clock".

One thing time does do for us is that it is consistent and an equal opportunist. It does not matter whether you are rich, poor, or middle-class. Time will give each of us 24 hours a day, 7 days a week, 4 to 5 weeks a month, and 12 months a year. Now how consistent is that!

My suggestion is to be time's friend. The best way to befriend time is preparation and planning. Here are some scenarios of our daily lives and suggestions of how to do some things differently to manage stress.

Scenario 1

You know what time you have to be at work, how long it takes for you to get ready, and how long the commute, but for some reason time always gets the best of you.

Suggestions

• First, prepare the night before by laying out what you are going to wear the next day.

- Next, take a shower at night instead of the morning.

- Third, if you have children, lay their clothes out the night before; prepare their lunches at night; place their book bags front at the door.

- Plan to leave 15 minutes earlier usual to prepare for unexpected delays in traffic

Scenario 2

"I never get enough sleep." "I am so tired." "I need to exercise so I can have some energy."

Suggestions

- Take a nice hot bath, grab a book, or listen to some soothing music, then set the alarm clock and watch yourself drift off to slumber land.

- Make a commitment to exercise daily (or a least 3 times a week) Set a reasonable schedule for exercise that usually no one can possibly interrupt and stick to it!

Stress Management

I want you to understand that we may not be able to eliminate all life's stressors but we can manage them. There is always a better way. We must identify the stressor, analyze the factors that cause stressful situations and provide solutions. Now here is one of the best stress relievers of all. I have saved it for last; it is called **"Friends"**. Surround yourself with true, loving friends who have the following characteristics:

- Supportive

- Positive

- Honest

- Understanding

- Empathetic

- Excellent listener

Remember also the important of organization in your life. Organizational skills:

- Plan

- Prioritize

- Analyze

You are the one who can control and manage the stress levels in your life. Consider the following:

- YOU decide how you are going to live your life

- Only YOU can control how you will react to a stressful situation

- Take time for yourself

- Meditate or pray

- Rest

Final Activity

Complete the following sentence:

When faced with a stressful situation I will manage it by:

_____

_____

Be blessed and not stressed! YOU can learn to manage the stress in your life.

Notes:

_____

_____

_____

_____

_____

_____

_____

_____

_____

_____

_____

_____

_____

_____

_____

_____

_____

_____

_____

_____

_____

_____

ABOUT THE AUTHOR

CHLOE D. MERRILL, PH.D., CFCS, CFLE

Dr. Chloe D. Merrill is the owner of Transformational Symmetry Consulting, LLC, which is a team of specialists trained in personal and corporate effectiveness. Founded in 1996 to inspire, motivate and guide individuals and organizations through "Continuous Change with Balance", Transformational Symmetry Consulting, LLC, links together the mind, body, and spirit to help improve productivity, creativity, memory, energy, ability to communicate with yourself and others, and overall improve quality of life.

Chloe is a Professor at Weber State University, Moyes College of Education, Department of Child and Family Studies. Chloe served as Department Chair from 1987 to 1995. She is certified in Family and Consumer Sciences (CFCS), a Certified Family Life Educator (CFLE), as well as certified to teach Secondary and Early Childhood Education.

Chloe is a member and active in numerous professional organizations. She is affiliated with civic and educational associations where she has or is currently serving as a board and committee member. Some include: Professional Woman Network, an international consulting organization; National Association of Female Executives; National Council on Family Relations; and the American Association of Family and Consumer Sciences. As a motivational speaker, conference and workshop lecturer, Chloe strives to educate all participants with knowledge that will help them throughout their lives.

Chloe has received numerous awards. Some include: Meritorious Service Award, National Council on Family Relations, 2001; Special Recognition award for Outstanding Service to the AAFCS Business Section, American Association of Family and Consumer Sciences, 1999; Outstanding Service to the Certified Family Life Educator Program Award, National Council on Family Relations, 1998; Lowe Innovative Teaching Award, Weber State University, 1998; Leader Award, American Association of Family and Consumer Sciences, 1998; Leader Award, Utah Association of Family and Consumer Sciences, 1997; and the Endowed Scholar for the College of Education, Weber State University from 1993-1997.

Chloe is a co-author in the books *Self-Esteem and Empowerment for Women, You're on Stage! Image, Etiquette, Branding & Style.* and *Women's Journey to Wellness: Mind, Body, & Spirit* published by the Professional Woman Publishing. Chloe's next book is entitled *Women as Leaders: Strategies for Empowerment & Communication.*

Chloe was born in Carbon County, Utah. She graduated with an Associates Degree from College of Eastern Utah, Bachelors and Master Degree from Utah State University, and Doctorate from Colorado State University. She and/or her team of specialists are available for presentations on a local, national, and international basis.

Contact
Transformational Symmetry Consulting, LLC
P.O. Box 150064
Ogden, UT 84415
Phone/Fax: 801-392-7465
http://transformationalsymmetry.com
E-mail: Transformationalsymmetry@comcast.net

EIGHTEEN

ROAD MAP TO TRANSFORMING LIFE'S PATHWAYS

By Chloe D. Merrill

There is a popular song written by Tom Cochrane that says, "Life is a highway; I want to ride it all night long." Life *is* a journey, which sometimes takes you flying on the highway, stopping and starting on city streets that only go one way, or slow and steady on country roads. Regardless of which type of road you find yourself on, you will be faced with a number of beginnings and endings. Each time we make a choice in life or deal with life's surprises, positive or negative, we face transitions that can be a beginning, an end, or both. Knowing where you have been, where you are going, and how you plan to get there, can make the journey much smoother and more enjoyable.

Sometimes life feels like a road race. At times, you are in the lead and things are going great. At other times, everyone is passing you by, and you cannot understand why. Or even worse, you are stuck on one-way streets that keep you going in circles. There are all sorts of opportunities presented and so many different roads you can take, and yet you have only a vague idea of where you are trying to go. Many times you choose a road that seems all right at the time, but in fact turns out to be a dead end, or takes you some place you really do not want to be.

In all areas of life there are new routes or pathways to be taken, but which is the right one? The road of life is strewn with obstacles, and there are a variety of issues being dealt with simultaneously, but the trick is finding ways to navigate those problems with creative solutions. When all other factors fall away, no matter how much you procrastinate, or blame someone or something else, you are the one that has to live with your choices. To help you stay on track, you need a life road map designed by and for you.

If you were going to drive to somewhere unfamiliar – whether cross-country or just across the city – what would be the first thing you would do? Map it out? And then after you mapped it out, would you never look at the map again? Not likely. More likely, you would refer to the map or directions often, to make sure that you were on the right track. You would be able to tell quickly if you needed to make adjustments, correct a mistake, or consider a change of plans.

Many different people and life experiences influence your road map of life. These past experiences, combined with your personal strengths and weaknesses, have created your unique life shape. You cannot turn back the clock and change your past; however, you can learn from it, so that you can change or direct your future. Your personal life map is unique to you and will give you a clear and deep understanding of yourself, your power, and your potential. This road map of your life is both an historical record and a creative tool for visioning the future.

Few of us can take the time to reflect on our life by writing an entire autobiography, but drawing a life road map can provide you with the same benefits. Once you have created your life map, you will need to have rest stops or "way stations" where you can pause to consult your maps, ask for directions, find a guide, and reflect on where you are going. When you first create your personal life road map, you will notice patterns emerging that include detours, successes and failures.

You will use a map to answer the most important questions: Where have I been? Where am I? Where am I going?

Activity: My Personal Life Road Map

• You are the mapmaker.

• Tools you will need:

    o Any large piece of paper;

    o An assortment of pens, colored pencils and colored felt-tipped markers (These will give you a good variety of writing tools to choose from.)

• Skills you need:

    o Your memory and imagination

There are no rules about what your map should look like.

Your life road map is the lifeline that the path your life has taken, or will take. It can be expressed as a straight line, a series of steps, a spiral, or any freeform design you choose. Show the ups and downs of your life, the forks in the road (major decisions), and the roads not taken (things you did not do). You can use symbols, pictures, and words to mark important events.

Example of Road Map of Life

Be sure to include hills, curves, crossroads, bumpy parts, and smooth parts. You can use words, picture, icons, or anything you would like.

(This is just an examples and not a real life person.)

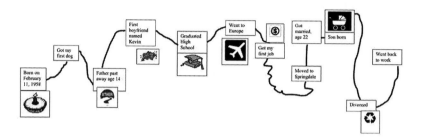

How much time you spend on the map is up to you. Do not feel rushed or hassled. Set it aside, and then come back to it. Remember, as you visualize your past, there is no right or wrong way to look at your life.

Some Ideas Of Symbols To Use:

Now create your future road map.

- Begin with the present moment and end with your passing or death.

- Be bold, dream big dreams.

- Explore alternative futures that emphasize different aspects of you.

- Express the deepest, wildest, most creative dreams you can focus on.

Now that you have your map, it is time for reflection.

- What have been the important moments in your life so far?

- Can you identify experiences that made you who you are?

- When did you meet the important people in your life?

- How will all of these moments help you in your future journey on this road map of life?

Change

As you move along your road map of life, you will find that your dreams change, your life changes, opportunities change, children grow and have different needs, and the journey changes. Your life roads do have contours. These contours can create special challenges or dangers, and also opportunities. Do not be afraid of the contours. The Chinese character for "crisis" includes the symbols for both "danger" and "opportunity."

It is dangerous to stagnate and avoid change, as this can lead to missed or lost opportunities. Search for opportunities everywhere. Search for opportunities to grow and expand, to laugh and love, to do kind things, and to learn from others. Search for opportunities to become the very finest person you can be. Search for opportunities to give to others, and to receive, for both are great blessings. Change can be difficult for a lot of people. The main thing to remember about change is: Change is inevitable, change is freedom, change is life.

The life map you created can help you to know the direction you want your life to go, which can guide you to handle the changes or transitions in your life so that you are growing and learning the way you want to. In life, there are times when things move slowly and do not seem to change very much. Then, suddenly, things change quickly; these are your life transitions.

Transitions are a natural process. Many transitions emerge from positive experiences or happy life events. Marriage, a new job, moving to a new city, birth of a child, leaving for college, re-acquaintance with an old friend – these events, which may be planned and expected, lead to a transition in our road map of life. At times, transitions are thrust upon us dramatically and unexpectedly. Accidents, death of loved ones (including pets), divorce, loss of a job, an illness – all of these events mean that we must leave something behind and then adjust to a new way of living, even if we feel totally unprepared to do so. These events can strike without warning and leave us in a personal crisis characterized by denial, anger, mourning, and withdrawal. Life transitions are challenging because they force us to let go of the familiar and face the future with a feeling of vulnerability. Transitions give us a chance to learn about our strengths and to explore what we really want out of life. This time of reflection can result in a sense of renewal, stability, and a new equilibrium.

Hints to Help Make the Transition Process Rewarding.

Life transitions are often difficult, but they have a positive side, too. They provide you with an opportunity to assess the direction your life is taking. They are a chance to grow and learn. Here are some ideas that may help make the process rewarding.

Blaze New Trails: Accept That Change Is a Normal Part of Life.

People, who accept that change is a normal part of life, seem to have the easiest time getting through life's transitions. Every change that occurs during your life is part of your personal development. The relationships in your life are in a constant state of change; whether it is a friendship, a marriage, or a parent/child relationship. As each person in the relationship grows, matures, and life circumstances change, they become different individuals. Sometimes as you mature, you or the person you share the relationship with will want different things from life, and come to realize that those in your life, even though they are growing and changing too, may no longer fit who each of you has become.

Rest Stops: Give Yourself Time to Heal and Reflect.

When your life is disrupted, hold on to those parts of your life that provide comfort and security. Keep as much of your daily routine as consistent as you can. Give yourself the needed time to work through the transition you are experiencing. When you are ready to move forward, look at your personal life map to see if it is still going to take you where you want to or had planned to go and make the necessary changes to your map by following your values and goals. Protect your time so that healing and reflection can take place. Some simple steps to protect your time are:

- Find a place where you can just "be", and go there daily at a set time.

- Post "Office/Home hours" when meetings, both at work and at home, can take place.

- Use an answering machine; you can return messages when you have time.

- Abolish your open-door policy; close your door.

- Let people know about your "time" intentions.

Map or GPS System: Identify Your Values and Life Goals.

Knowing what your values and goals in life are helps you to understand who you are and what you want from life. With your values and goals in place, you may see the transition as just another life challenge. There are many different values people want to pursue on their life journey.

The two main types of values on our road map are Core Values and Satellite Values. Core Values are the mirror of your personality, and are central to defining who you are as a person. While your knowledge, attitudes, and beliefs strongly influence who you are, it is your values that are the foundation that the other facets are built on. Some examples of Core Values are:

- Children

- Country

- Freedom

- Money

- Religion

- Spouse

Surrounding your core values are the Satellite Values that you hold dear, but you are not as strongly committed to. Satellite values are less important to you and more open to compromise and change. Some examples of Satellite Values are:

- Beauty

- Cultural interests

- Friends

- Hobbies

- Intelligence

- Political views

- Recreational pursuits

- Sports

- Work

When you are being true to yourself, your goals will be directly related to your values. Your goals can be as lofty as you would like; however, you also need to have realistic goals that are within reach. Realistic goals can help you make progress towards your loftier goals. By setting realistic goals, you guarantee yourself a better chance of success.

Goals are based on action, and to realize your goals you need to take action. You have to be willing to do the work. When you reach your goals, it enhances your self-esteem and motivates you to set bigger and more difficult goals.

Activity: Values and Goals Identification

On the inside of the circle list your Core Values and around the outside list your Satellite Values.

Values Wheel

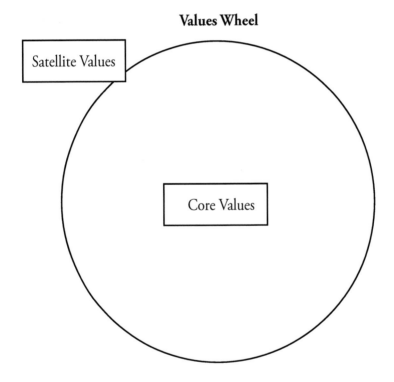

Now that you have your values outlined, list at least 3 goals that you have and the action steps that are needed to complete these goals.

Goal and Action Planning

Goal	Action Steps
	• •
	• •
	• •

Potholes: Recognize Emotions are Part of the Process.

Whenever changes occur in your life, it is impossible to undergo them without your emotions being involved. It is normal to feel insecure, happy, sad, or anxious, to name a few emotions. These feelings plus numerous others are part of the process. Daniel Goleman, in his book *Emotional Intelligence,* defines an emotion as "a feeling, and its distinctive thoughts, psychological and biological states, and range of propensities to act." It is essential to be aware of your emotional responses and allow them to become part of each transition.

Emotions range from positive to negative within you. You do not always have the power to choose what happens to you or the emotional response that those happenings will arouse within you, but you do have the power to choose how you allow the transitions and associated emotions to affect you in the long run. It is what you do with or about the emotions that affect you the most. How you react is your choice; you have the power.

Scenic Routes: Stop and Smell the Roses.

Take care of yourself. Times of transition can be very stressful, even if the transition is good. Some important points to remember are:

- Be sure to do something for yourself every day.

- Get plenty of sleep.

- Eat healthy meals and snacks.

- Exercise every day, even if it is just a short 20-minute walk.

- Be sure to spend time by yourself.

- Read a book that you have been wanting to read.

- Meditate

- Get a massage, pedicure, manicure, or better yet all three.

Break Through the Barriers: Develop a Good Support System.

Have a good support system that understands what you want and are willing and able to support you in your journey. Examples of support systems are:

- Children

- Colleagues

- Friends

- Mentor

- Professional coach

- Professional therapist

- Spouse

Support systems can provide you with different kinds of support. Some of these kinds are:

- Emotional support, where you can confide in someone and know that you will be loved and cared about. This is support that you can lean on, and it can help boost your self-esteem.

- Belonging support gives you the feeling that you "fit in." It is the belief that you are not alone, and that you have company through the transition.

- Informational support is when you need advice, information, or feedback that will help you solve the challenge.

- Tangible support is helpful when you need assistance with a job, or require aid, a gift, or a loan. This support is also good when you cannot handle the situation on your own.

Roadblocks: "Woulda-Coulda-Shouldas"

Get rid of all the "woulda-coulda-shouldas." You cannot live your life based on what you or others think you "would, could or should" do. You need to live your life based on what is possible and feels right for you. Discover what you want and what you are good at, and take actions designed to fulfill your potential. You might have preconceived notions or have already figured how things should be, could be, or ought to be. You set out to travel where you think you need to go, and in the process you block out other avenues, possibilities, or interesting sites that you might have otherwise seen or experienced if it were not for the "woulda-coulda-shoulda" blinders that you put on your life. Remove them from your life and break through the roadblocks you or others have given you.

Trust in your own ability to see your way through the transitions. Remember, on the road of life you will have curves and turns, new roads and scenic routes, as well as potholes and roadblocks, but your road map to transforming your life pathways will continue to move forward. Enjoy your life and the journey.

The following poem nicely sums up looking at the Road Map to Transforming Life's Pathways.

Life's Journey
By An Anonymous Author

Do not undermine your worth by comparing yourself with others.
It is because we are different that each of us is special.
Do not set your goals by what other people deem important.
Only you know what is best for you.
Do not take for granted the things closest to your heart.
Cling to them as you would your life; for without them, life is meaningless.

Do not let your life slip through your fingers by living in the past, nor for the future.

By living your life one day at a time, you live all of the days of your life.

Do not give up when you still have something to give.

Nothing is really over until the moment you stop trying.

It is a fragile thread that binds us to each other.

Do not be afraid to encounter risks.

It is by taking chances that we learn how to be brave.

Do not shut love out of your life by saying it is impossible to find.

The quickest way to receive love is to give love.

The fastest way to lose love is to hold it too tightly.

In addition, the best way to keep love is to give it wings.

Do not dismiss your dreams.

To be without dreams is to be without hope.

To be without hope is to be without purpose.

Do not run through life so fast that you forget not only where you have been, but also where you are going.

Life is not a race, but a journey to be savored each step of the way.

Recommended Reading/References

Actualizations: You Don't Have to Rehearse to Be Yourself by Stewart Emery

Ageless Body, Timeless Mind by Deepak Chopra

Emotional Intelligence by Daniel Goleman

Living with Change: Positive Techniques for Transforming Your Life by Ursula Markham

Moving Through Life Transitions with Power and Purpose by Cara DiMarco

Now What? 90 Days to a New Life Direction by Laura Berman Fortgang

Power of Intention by Wayne Dyer

Power of Now by Eckhart Tolle

The Art of Possibility: Transforming Professional and Personal Life by Rosamund Stone Zander and Benjamin Zander

The Four Agreements: A Practical Guide to Personal Freedom by Don Miguel Ruiz

What Color is Your Parachute? by Richard Bolles

Websites
- http://www.tickle.com

- http://www.ivillage.com

- http://lifemap.eons.com/

Notes:

_____

_____

_____

_____

_____

_____

_____

_____

_____

_____

_____

_____

_____

_____

_____

_____

_____

_____

_____

ABOUT THE AUTHOR

VIOLET MATHIS

Violet Mathis is President and CEO of The V Factor. She specializes in international workshops, seminars and coaching for self empowerment. Her background is in dentistry and has been a Registered Dental Hygienist for thirty years. Opening her own management consulting company in 2000, Violet is a certified consultant for Bent Erickson & Associates, employment law and human resource specialties, and well as IPM (Integrated Performance Management). She also is a member of SCN (Speaking and Consulting Network as well as ADMC (Academy of Dental Management Consultants). She is a member of NAFE (National Association of Female Executives) and was the Governor of Who's Who International.

Violet has lived overseas and is an international author and speaker. She is certified in Women's Diversification Issues. She has worked in the healthcare field, interior design, sales, and is forever volunteering for various social organizations.

Violet Mathis has a passion for people. She always sees the best in each person and has the ability to bring out their bests qualities.. She loves to travel and is always eager for more knowledge. Having a positive attitude is of the utmost importance in her life.

Contact
The V Factor
vlmathis@bellsouth.net

NINETEEN

THE ART OF FORGIVENESS

By Violet Mathis

It is difficult to understand the word "forgiveness" if you are in pain or angry. It could be as simple as forgiving the person who cut you off in traffic, the random act of a killer gone mad and someone you love being at the wrong place at the wrong time, the parent who left you when you were a child, the spouse who abused you, or the sexual abuse when you were a child. Throughout our lifetime and almost on a daily basis, we are placed into situations where we have the opportunity to forgive someone or something. How we react to and handle these situations will determine the quality of life and happiness or pain we derive from each situation.

By definition, forgiveness is the mental, emotional, and/or spiritual process of ceasing to feel resentment or anger against another person for a perceived offense, difference or mistake, or ceasing to demand punishment or restitution. It is a legitimate and complete act by an individual, even though it may or may not lead to reconciliation.

Forgiveness is not easy. It can be very difficult, whether due to hurtful words or hateful thoughts. It also is clearly a gift we give ourselves. We must first consciously decide and want to forgive, since it does not come automatically. If we think about it, forgiveness is a selfish act, because the benefits to us are much greater than to the one being forgiven.

Please understand that forgiving is not the same as forgetting. There are as many ways of defining forgiveness as there are of defining love. Forgiveness does not just happen without first consciously wanting and choosing to forgive. It truly becomes a journey in one's life. As we proceed through this process, we will encounter many feelings and emotions along the way. In the end, we will be the recipient of the empowering feeling. Forgiveness does not mean forgetting, and forgetting is not the issue as to whether we forgive. Dr. Phil McGraw says, "You have the power to be miserable for the rest of your life, or you can say, 'I'm going to give myself permission to heal.'" The decision is yours as to whether you choose to remove the roadblocks and continue to move forward, or stand still.

As we think of the many ways we can forgive, we find there are many myths regarding the process. Some of the myths are:

- I have probably already forgiven him or her.

- If I forgive, I would be letting that person off the hook.

- I should forgive only if that person apologizes.

- Offering forgiveness implies that what the other person did was okay.

- If I do not forgive, then the other person suffers.

All of these are the result of inward thinking, and ultimately only hurt YOU. The best thing we as individuals can do is to understand the steps of forgiveness, and the reason it is so important to begin the process. In getting started, there are basically five steps for us to take:

1. Recognize that there is a hurt or violation against you.

2. Know that it is not your fault.

3. Choose to forgive.

4. Begin the process of forgiveness.

5. Move forward with your life.

The first step to freedom from the hurt will be in confronting the emotional pain, and realizing that the pain, injustice, or grief actually exists. The unfairness of the situation needs to be acknowledged before we are able to move on with our lives. We must open our heart and mind before we can actually heal the pain.

Acknowledging that you were truly not at fault for the injustice that happened to you opens up the format for inner peace and promotes inner healing. New studies show that anger and resentment double the chance of myocardial heart attacks in women with previous coronary problems. Other studies indicate that cancer and other deadly illnesses are also caused by anger and resentment. Stress is definitely associated with harboring anger, hurt, and feelings that cause negative thoughts, and keep us from realizing our true happiness in life. So as you can see, medical implications definitely promote a case for healthy feelings and letting go of excess baggage by acknowledging forgiveness.

There are also many health reasons for forgiveness. A few of these are:

- Reduced stress

- Better heart health

- Stronger relationships

- Reduced pain

- Greater happiness

- "Age-erasers", especially for women

Once we realize that forgiveness must be a deliberate decision on our part, we then are able to move forward with the process. The decision to forgive is definitely not easy, but is essential for growth and healing within ourselves. Deciding to let go of the injustices, anger, or hurt moves you from the "**victim**" **stage** to the **healing state**. The concept of thinking that if you let go of these feelings, it somehow releases the other person from blame will only continue to hurt you. Forgiveness does not care whether the other person asks for your forgiveness or acknowledges any wrongdoing. Being willing to forgive is a very courageous move on your part. It literally enables you to begin the healing process and possibly see the other person differently. Consider their background and circumstances, and perhaps begin to see the other person in a different light. What they did cannot be justified, but just maybe they deserve some compassion for their issues in life. Remember, it is not about the other person; it is about healing yourself.

Once you begin the process of forgiveness, there is much to be learned. Just deciding to forgive is the initial step. The second step might be to read stories of other's forgiveness, or to begin journaling your feelings just to get them out and into perspective of how you really feel. You might think of talking to a therapist to guide you along in your process. In many instances, just to hear another perspective helps us. If you believe in a Higher Power, pray and enlist help and support with the process. Realize it may take a long time and a lot of work to forgive, as your issues may stem from childhood. Some wounds have been in existence for a long time. Remember that no matter how long the process takes, you are working toward total health and happiness. And let's face it, isn't that what we are all looking for ultimately?

Once the decision has been made to forgive and the process has begun, then you will you be able to move forward and reach your goal of true happiness where you have control of your own emotions. It is a conscious decision to heal and liberate yourself, no matter what the other person did or chooses to do. These acts are not only empowering, but are truly skills with which you can have a better and brighter life. We should remember that it is all about giving ourselves permission to move forward.

On the other side of the coin, it is about asking for our own forgiveness. Sometimes we make mistakes for which we need forgiveness. When we do this, we could possibly be holding ourselves up to unrealistic expectations.

If we are truly honest with ourselves, we have to admit that there really is not a lot of true forgiveness in our world. Religions have taught forgiveness for centuries. Within the different religious faiths, there are varying beliefs of how forgiveness is attained. These may be something that you as a reader would wish to study, depending upon your faith. Just to highlight a few:

- **Buddhism**: Forgiveness is seen as a practice to prevent harmful emotions from causing havoc on one's mental well-being. Buddhists believe that feelings of ill will and resentment have a lasting effect on the mind Karma, and that it is not a matter of seeking revenge, but of practicing metta and forgiveness. The victimizer is really the unfortunate one.

- **Christianity**: According to Christian teachings, forgiveness is the basis of spiritual teachings. Since God is considered the original source of forgiveness through the sacrifice of his son Jesus, Christians are expected to practice forgiveness with others. By forgiving others, the person becomes free.

  o Roman Catholic and Orthodox Christian churches teach that the church mediates forgiveness. In Anglican churches, one must confess their sins to a priest and obtain absolution as a formal expression of God's forgiveness

  o Protestant denominations teach that a believer receives forgiveness more directly through a sincere expression of repentance to God. They, in turn, should continue with forgiveness of others.

- **Hinduism**: The concept of atonement for one's wrongdoing and asking for forgiveness is an extremely important part of Hinduism. The effects of the present and future experiences make one responsible for one's own life and the pain in others.

- **Islam**: Forgiveness is a prerequisite for true and or genuine peace. Islam teaches that God is the most forgiving, and is the original source of forgiveness. The Quar'an occasionally gives Muslims the right to portray violent behavior, which has been seen as condoning unforgiving behavior. The Quar'an actually goes into great detail about who can and cannot be forgiven.

- **Judaism:** If a person harms another, but then sincerely and honestly apologizes to the wronged individual and tries to rectify the wrong, the wronged individual is religiously required to grant forgiveness. If the wrongdoer does not apologize, there is no religious obligation to grant forgiveness.

As you can see, all spiritual organizations believe in some form of forgiveness. The Bible is filled with verse after verse. In most religious teachings, there is an underlying basis for many modern day practices and traditions of forgiveness. Religious forgiveness is being questioned by many scientific disciplines such as the psychology, sociology, and medicine entities. Ongoing studies will be inevitable throughout time, and we probably will be at the same juncture as we are now.

It is amazing that in our society we condone or forgive many things. We forgive debts for loan programs such as student loans, we forgive tardiness, minor indiscretions, our children for playing pranks, our spouse for forgetting the milk at the store, and we forgive on a daily basis for many relatively trivial issues. For the most part, we really do not think of these as real problems. When it comes to really important issues, we have much more difficulty trying to forgive, whether it is forgiveness of ourselves, or others.

In learning to forgive ourselves, remember that we are all human, and must accept ourselves for who we are with all our faults. Being human means that we make mistakes each day! Letting go of past failures and mistakes is the beginning of self-forgiveness. Sometimes it is easier to forgive someone else, even for heinous crimes, easier than it is for one to forgive oneself; but forgiveness of ourselves is imperative. We actually tend to hold ourselves more accountable than the other person. Sometimes we feel guilty for things that we had no control over. Whether we were seduced as a child before we were too young to even know, or whether it was something catastrophic like September 11, 2001, it is difficult to let go of past offenses.

You might begin this quest for self-forgiveness by asking yourself several questions:

1. What is self-forgiveness?

2. What does it feel like to believe there is no penance for your mistake?

3. Have you ever made a mistake and then forgiven yourself for it?

4. How did the forgiveness of that event make you feel?

5. What blocks you from forgiving yourself?

6. Do you need help or new tools in order for self-forgiveness?

7. What would happen if you forgave yourself?

8. Does spirituality play a part in your self-forgiveness?

9. How would you feel if you did not carry around that weight?

10. Could you accept true inner peace without the turmoil?

11. Why are you continuing to hold on to the anger or self-destructive behavior?

12. If I forgave myself, what would happen to my emotional being?

13. Do I truly want to forgive myself?

14. Do I deserve to be forgiven?

Some of these questions may sound silly or even obvious to you, because you are saying "Of course I want to be free of feeling guilt or of feeling like a failure!" Unfortunately, we continue to beat up on ourselves, and believe that there is no point, or that we do not deserve to feel whole and emotionally stable.

Now that we have an idea of what we a looking for, let's see how we go about it.

- Make a list of the mistake, misdeed, crime, or belief for which you are unable to forgive yourself.

- How much energy or emotional stress is consumed by this event?

- What actual feelings does this event evoke?

- Why do you feel so strongly about this event?

- Who was responsible for the event?

- Do you blame that person for your guilt feelings?

- How often does this event arise?

- How would you describe your role in this event?

- Do you feel you were the victim, perpetrator, enabler, martyr, bystander, instigator, target, scapegoat, distracter, peacemaker, people pleaser, or rescuer?

- Who was responsible for you harboring this burden?

- Who was the enabler for your guilt feelings?

- How can you get past this and forgive yourself?

- Do you want to be forgiven?

Some of these questions will evoke many feelings, which may have not surfaced or have been squelched for a long time. So, please be prepared for this, know that it is a good thing, and that moving forward requires facing the past, even when it hurts. Self-recovery is not always painless. Forgiveness is about forgiving people, not their behaviors. Self-forgiveness can be an extraordinary act of healing yourself mentally, emotionally and spiritually. The results will be apparent in your daily life, not only to you, but also to others around you.

Whether you need to forgive others or to forgive yourself, today is literally the first day of the rest of your life. How you choose to move forward depends on you. There are many resources for those who truly wish to get help and promote true happiness. It definitely is an art, since you must begin with one stroke, and continue to embellish with color and stroke after stroke. The final picture will be a work of art, and you are the main subject on the canvas. Let's move forward with all the color and beauty of a Degas or a Picasso. You deserve to be happy, healthy, and definitely full of living color. Remember, art increases in value over time, just as we as individuals do.

Recommended Reading

Forgiveness: How to Make With Your Past and Get On With Your Life by Dr. Sidney B. Simon.

How to Forgive When You Can't Forget by Charles Klein.

ABOUT THE AUTHOR

PATRICIA A. CHEESEBORO

Patricia A. Cheeseboro is the President and CEO of Cheeseboro Consulting Services, which is dedicated to inspiring and motivating professional and personal growth in individuals and organizations through workshops, seminars and whole-life coaching.

Patricia has worked for over sixteen years as a caseworker with the Commonwealth of Pennsylvania Department of Public Welfare, and has a strong background in case management, counseling, and writing individual plans for self-sufficiency. Ms. Cheeseboro earned a Bachelor of Science degree from Pennsylvania State University in Individual and Family Studies, in 1980. She is a Certified Consultant and Trainer with The Professional Woman Network (PWN), specializing in Professional Development and Youth Issues.

She is the wife of Andrew Cheeseboro and the mother of three daughters — Jasmine, Amber, and Nia. She is inspired by her family members who allow her to pursue her passion in helping others.

Patricia has a passion for training and motivating others to be empowered and to realize their full potential in spite of their circumstances. Here motto is "I can do all things through Christ who strengthens me." (Philippians 4:13) Patricia is a highly=capable consultant and inspiring speaker, providing services both nationally and internationally.

Contact
Cheeseboro Consulting Services
P.O. Box 15586
Pittsburgh, PA 15244
(412) 965-0418
PACheeseboro@aol.co
www.protrain.net

TWENTY

FROM NEGATIVE TO POSITIVE: CHANGING YOUR PERSPECTIVE ON LIFE

By Patricia Cheeseboro

How do you change your perspective on life and move from negative to the positive? The answer is "thinking positively". "Think positive" are the buzzwords; if you have a positive attitude you can expect positive life. If you think positive and have the positive mental attitude then you should have peace, success, improved relationships, better health, happiness and satisfaction. Sounds simple enough! *Does just "thinking" positively changes your perspective on life?* The answer to the question is *no*. Not only do you have to think positive, you have to take action to become positive. In order to take action, one must make a daily commitment to achieve this state of mind and attitude, which requires constructive changes in one's life.

Before you can begin to take the necessary action to change, you must first look at how you perceive life now. Your perception is based on your past experiences (both good and bad) which ultimately shapes your reality. Each of us has been asked the famous question, "Is your glass is half empty or half full? Believe it or not, there is soundness in this question and your answer is important in relationship to your life perception. It actually determines whether in our minds that we are successful or unsuccessful.

The "half empty" answer would mean you have a more negative perception; and of course the "half full" that you have a more positive perception. Trying to keep the "half full" perception gets tough because negative issues face us every day when you read the newspaper, watch the news, listen to complaining co-workers and customers, grumpy fast food workers, are involved in a divorce, watch gas prices rising daily, read about the War in Iraq and the list goes and on. But you can remove some of the world negativity from time to time! For instance, I am currently on a boycott from the news; that is how I try to remove some of the day-to-day negativity from my life. I do this every few months because this type of negativity can destroy your spirit and faith.

Negativity is contagious; it actually kills and destroys our hopes and dreams. It creates discouragement and eventually brings about defeat; it can leave you without motivation and enthusiasm. Negativity can bring an end to many relationships; if it is not handled and removed from your way of thinking, the negativity may consumes you and will attract other negative people who will affirm and give power to your negative thoughts and words.

Imagine a bag of potatoes with one rotten potato. As that one rotten potato decays, it usually starts in the core and spreads to outside. Once the decay reaches the outside every potato it touches starts decaying until the whole bag is decayed. When you open the pantry with the rotten potatoes, what a foul smell will greet you! Believe it or not, the same thing happens with people, **negativity stinks**! You have to remove yourself from pessimistic people and negative environments or soon you, too, will carry the label and stench.

On the other hand, if you notice a potato that is rotten on the outside, you quickly remove it from the bag. The other potatoes will continue to flourish and thrive; you may even notice new growth (until you change them into french fries or mashed potatoes!) The same holds true if you are positive; you have to be around other positive people. They will provide encouragement and motivation to help you flourish and grow. You have to remove negative people from around yourself before you get contaminated.

Unlike the potatoes in the bag, you have the power to remove self from around negative people and situations. You are in control of your thoughts and words, which leads you to "thinking positive". But in order to transform to the "think positive", you got to find the underlying negative habits and or emotions that are the causes of your own fears, insecurities and weakness.

The first thing we must realize is that oftentimes if something bad happens, we want to place the blame on someone else or life circumstances such as social economic status, gender, ethnicity, family ancestry and race. We may even blame God for our problems. In reality it may be a case of **hidden self-sabotage** such as fear of success or failure, procrastination, holding on to feelings of guilt and blame, or lack of self-confidence.

Self-sabotaging issues develop over time and may cause us to have a negative perception of life.

How do you learn exactly *how* you are self-sabotaging? Purchase a journal and keep track daily (for two weeks) of how you look at life " half-full" or "half-empty". For fourteen days, you are going to examine your life from the outside looking in. Also, note as to who the main characters were in your life on each specific day. How did you respond to them? How did they contribute to your attitude? Did they sabotage you? Each day, make notes about your fears, weaknesses, and self-talk. Review the journal after fourteen days, and determine if there is a pattern to your thinking.

This is a challenge because you need to **identify** the bad habit, **expose** it and **transform** it. Personal renewal often begins with small adjustments that launch the way for massive change. When trying to break old habits, do begin with small steps, which in turn create immeasurable rewards; as you change one habit, this makes other positive changes in areas of your life. Once you have identified and thus exposed the self-sabotage habit, you want to transform every area of your life: career, relationships, spirituality, financial and health/ wellness. What self-sabotage habit is affecting all areas of your life? The self-sabotage that is affecting **all areas of life** is where you want to start your first.

Exercise

'**Transformation: 21 Day Challenge**' begins with your list of self-sabotage habits you have discovered from your 14 days of journal writing. Choose one negative habit; you will then write strategies as to how you will begin to break this habit. Put these strategies into your life for the next twenty-one days and allow your new behaviors to take hold.

What is the one habit that is affecting every area of your life?

For example: Procrastination

Health/Wellness: I will begin walking each day at lunchtime for 20 minutes.

Financial: I will open a support savings account and direct deposit $50/pay.

Career: Devote 60 minutes each evening on business/planning goals.

Relationship: Family meal together at least twice a week.

Spirituality: Spend 20 minutes before dressing praying and mediating with God.

Keep notes in journal and record your progress for twenty-one days. Once completed, start your new challenge. It is important to focus on what is holding you back in life. It is time to reflect on your attitude and self-defeating behaviors. Ask yourself the following:

Questions:

- What can't I live the life, I have envisioned for myself?

- Why can't I have a good relationship?

- Why I can't get out of debt?

- My world seems to have turned upside down when am I going to get some relief?

- Why can't I get that promotion when I have the qualifications?

- Why can't I lose weight?

- Why do I feel so far away from my spirituality and God?

You may want to adjust your thoughts and words to positive thinking. Start talking to yourself by saying "I can change my life by changing my thinking". Take a look at your life and see how these tips and challenge help you to take the bigger challenge of living a more positive life.

Tips and challenges to moving from the negative to positive:

- **Start each day with prayer, mediation and praise.** Praise God no matter what you're going through. Also have a weekly affirmation or scriptures, use them so that can be part of your everyday self talk and speak out loud to others. My favorites are "I can do all things through Christ who strengthens me." Or "God did not give me a spirit of fear."

- **Write down your dreams and goals**; without a plan and purpose you will never reach success. Remember true success is not about money and material things; it is about finding your purpose, talents, and God's plan for your life. Not only write it down, but visualize it, rehearse in your mind and begin to act the part as if you have already obtained it. Believe that you have the job you desire or own your own company. Write down these thoughts and dreams. Chart your course.

- **Change your talk and thinking** as we often "breathe death" into our situations. Be very conscious of what you say and think. You'll be surprised how easily negative talk seeps into your daily conversation. "Speak life" into your situation and take charge of your thoughts. Keep a notebook with you and write down your negative words, rephrase them into positive. For example:

Death: " I **can't ever** get out of debt!"

Life: " I **will** get out of debt with budgeting and not using credit cards.

- **Surround yourself with positive people** who will motivate and give encouragement. If you surround yourself with people who constantly complain that nothing is ever right; before long you will find that you have become a complainer. Take note especially in your workplace because the workplace seems to breed complainers! Think about all the people who have influence your life and/or you admire them. Write out all the qualities they have that make them positive and successful.

- **Learn to love self.** Take time out and rediscover YOU. We often get so caught up trying to please others that we forget about self. There is a song that says, "I need some *me* time." Make the time for yourself.

- **Do not compare yourself to other people.** We often look at other people and have the tendency to overlook our own strengthens and talents. Thus, we focus on all our shortcomings and inabilities, what we haven't accomplished, or what we don't have. We often think that other's grass is much greener than ours, so we gather negative feelings such as envy or bitterness. Remember, you have your own unique talents and abilities!

- **Seek excellence, not perfection.** If you aim for the impossible; you become frustrated and defeated. Do your best in every area of your life and accept that it is human to fail and make mistakes; do not attempt to outdo others or give 150% of yourself on each project. No one is perfect. Do your best and no more. It is one thing to try for perfection, another to attempt excellence. Choose excellence.

- **Look for the positive in every situation**. You have to believe and have faith no matter what you are going through there is blessing waiting to unfold. When going through the storms of life, gently say, "This too shall pass." You have the choice of either looking at each situation in a positive way, or filling your mind with doom and defeat.

- **Find resources that will help you be more positive** or (help you to focus on "positive thinking" and clear your mind). Consider reading an inspirational book, listening to peaceful music, watching a good movie, or taking a warm bath. (I find that sitting by a lake, ocean, or stream is comforting to me.) Find your own quiet space so that you may relax your mind and focus on the good in life.

- **Live by your virtues.** Honesty, God-centeredness, fairness, patience, kindness, compassion, humility, responsibility, fairness, courage, self-discipline, obedience, generosity and respect are examples of virtues. Make a list of all your virtues and challenge them daily, as they are only true virtues if they are practiced and lived!

- **"I love you"** and **"Thank you"** are two phrases so many times have made a difference to me even in bad situations. Use these two phrases along with others such as, "You did a great job"; "You're wonderful", or "I appreciate you so much." Believe me, when you speak words of appreciation and encouragement it brings about a sense of joy, hope and healing. A few years ago I received a call from a friend, Julia, to inform me that she had leukemia. It was hard to find the right words, but I wanted to thank her for her kindness to me during our lifetime together; but I didn't want these words of appreciation to sound so "final". During our conversation, Julia opened the opportunity for me to share my thankfulness. (Julia had helped me to adjust to living in Philadelphia by showing me where to live. She had watched my children for me and had even given me the confidence to ride the subway). As we ended our conversation that day, I heard, "I love you." I had shared my appreciation for her; now she was sharing her thankfulness for me. Remember the importance of kind words.

- **Get rid of baggage**, clean it out and only leave behind the lessons learned. Take a piece of paper and look at your life closely; write down any hurts, mistakes or failures that are "personal bag" in your mind. Then get another piece of paper and write down on the lesson learned from each piece of baggage such as the importance of forgiveness, loving self, being responsible for your own life, increased self-confidence, and peace of mind. Tell yourself "The past is the *past;* it can no longer hurt me nor control me. I will not allow the past to destroy me or my dreams and goals. I will admit some have caused me to be a better person but I am removing this personal baggage because it has served its purpose." Take the list of your personal baggage and shred it. Let it go!

It is a challenge to move toward the idealism of "think positive". However, it is a necessary change to become a better you and more optimistic. Learn to see beyond your limits, problems, and challenges; focus on the positive outcomes and not the negative. Start by making small changes, which in turn will create immeasurable rewards as you transform into a positive person.

Take the necessary challenge in defining your life and knowing yourself. As your life takes *center stage* you will realize that there will be changes made to your *reality show* because of new experiences, growing older and wiser, people will coming and going; your life always gaining a new perspective Know what you're roles are and live daily by your virtues and values. Take control of yourself because you alone are responsible for your thoughts, words and actions. If you live each day by "think positive" idealism, you can accomplishment your goals and dreams.

Notes:

_____

_____

_____

_____

_____

_____

_____

_____

_____

_____

_____

_____

_____

_____

_____

_____

_____

_____

_____

_____

_____

ABOUT THE AUTHOR

RUBY M. ASHLEY, MBA

Ruby Ashley is Chief Executive Officer of Ruby Ashley & Associates. She is a leader in personal and professional development, specializing in the delivery of workshops, seminars, training programs, and assessments. Her workshops and training programs are highly interactive and stimulating with focus on improving employee performance. She firmly believes that as long as individuals are willing to learn, change, and grow, they will always reach high levels of achievement.

Ms. Ashley is an accomplished motivational keynote speaker, facilitator, trainer, and consultant with more than 26 years of experience in the corporate environment. As a Certified Customer Service Trainer, she delivers an outstanding Customer Service Excellence program. Other training program topics include: personal and professional development, women's issues, diversity and multiculturalism, self-esteem, leadership development, strategic planning, road map to retirement, and team building. Teen topics are Save Our Youth, Teen Image, and Leadership.

Ms. Ashley earned Bachelor's and Master's degrees in Business from Brenau University in Gainesville, GA. She is a member of The Professional Woman Network (PWN), is a certified trainer, and member of The PWN International Advisory Board. Ms. Ashley holds memberships in other professional organizations, including the American Business Woman Association, Toastmasters International, Les Brown Speaker's Bureau, and is an affiliate of Leadership Development Group, Inc. She is a youth mentor and an active volunteer in her community.

Ruby Ashley is also a co-author of *Becoming the Professional Woman, Self-Esteem & Empowerment for Women* and *The Young Woman's Guide for Personal Success* in the PWN Library.

Contact
Ruby Ashley & Associates
1735 Chatham Ridge Circle #206
Charlotte, NC 28273
(404) 316-5931
rbyash@aol.com
www.protrain.net

TWENTY-ONE

BECOME THE WOMAN YOU WANT TO BE

By Ruby Ashley

Dare To Dream

So how's your life? Has it somehow slipped away from what you always dreamed it would be? Or have you just accepted what life offered you, thinking you didn't have a choice? How do you feel at this very moment in your life? Are you happy, sad, fearful, determined, procrastinating, undecided, existing, standing still, waiting for a miracle, dreams on hold, dwelling on what could or should have been? Are you living the life you've always wanted to live, or are you not quite sure where you are in your life? One thing you must understand about life – it cannot be placed on hold, and it will not stand still to wait for us to get our acts together. We must be realistic with the fact that whatever our goals and dreams may be, we must move forward with an action plan. When your plans include a **desire** propelled by a **purpose**, complimented by a stronger **passion** for what you are doing, you will be well on your way to getting what you want.

The three crucial components that will help you achieve your dreams are defined as follows:

Desire - Long for; wish for; want strongly; an inclination to want things.

Purpose - Be intent on doing something; an anticipated outcome that guides your planned actions; your anticipation of an outcome that provided your reason for doing something.

Passion - Strong feeling or emotion; something that is desired intensely.

Do you remember when you were little, and people asked you what you wanted to be when you grew up? Do you remember responding with absolute confidence that you were going to be a ballerina or a pet doctor or an astronaut? The possibilities were endless, and you had no doubt you could achieve whatever you wanted. Unfortunately, somewhere along the way "reality" set in, and you stopped dreaming about who you could become. Maybe someone told you that you weren't skinny enough to be a ballerina, or that you weren't good enough in science to become a vet, or that only the "best of the best" could become astronauts. So you settled for different goals: motherhood, a good paying job, a happy marriage. While all of these things are admirable achievements, you may still feel something is missing. Maybe you still have a dream you would like to achieve, but now, with all the responsibilities of work and family, you don't know where you will find the time. You may feel like your life is just passing you by, and that you will never be able to become the woman you wanted to be when you were a little girl.

So many demands are placed on women today. Often we're expected to take care of the children, the cooking, the laundry, the dishes, and our husbands, all while holding down a full time job. It's no wonder we feel so tired all the time, and when we're tired, there is little energy left for thinking about, much less pursuing, our goals and dreams. But we owe it to ourselves and to our family to do what we need to do to be happy. And if that means spending less time with them in order to become a dancer or a doctor or an aerospace engineer, then we should do that. I know it may seem selfish, but unless we take care of ourselves and our wants first, then we will never be happy. Think about it, you are a role model for your kids. What kind of example do you want to set for them? Do you want to be someone who pursues her dreams and is happy, or do you want to be a person who sacrifices everything for her family, only to end up dissatisfied and unhappy with her life? Now, I'm not saying that dedicating yourself to your family isn't a worthwhile endeavor, and if that is your dream, I think you should pursue it just as strongly as you should any other career goal. What I am saying is that you shouldn't settle for the easy path in life because that is all you think you can achieve.

Right now, you have everything you need inside of you to live your dream. All you have to do is find your passion and then take the necessary steps to get there. The first step is to determine what you really love to do.

First and most of all, be the "authentic person" you are. Be honest and truthful with yourself; search way down deep in your heart to explore your feelings and what you really want out of life. Don't settle for just being accepted; let your gut feelings help you make the necessary choices you need to so that you can move forward. You are not counterfeit or copied. You are real and worthy of everything your heart desires. Don't be afraid of what you really want out of life because you feel your dream is so big that others will laugh at you or talk about you. Why? Because they will. Get ready. Some will love you, and some will hate you. Just keep moving forward and don't ever give up!

List one of your dreams or goals:

How strong is your desire to achieve your dream/goal?

What satisfaction will this dream or goal bring to you?

How will you use passion to achieve your dream or goal?

List 4 passionate steps you will take to achieve your dream or goal.
1. _____
2. _____
3. _____
4. _____

Congratulations! It's time to take action on the things you wrote. Get started now!

Take the dream or goal you listed above and think about it. Imagine the best possible thing that could happen if your endeavor was a great success. Close your eyes and try to experience it with all your senses. What does this achievement look and feel like? Are there any tastes or smells associated with the experience? What are some of comments you hear people saying about your success? These images will be what you have to hold onto when things get tough, and you run into the inevitable obstacles and challenges you will experience along the way to making your dreams or goals a reality. Remember, obstacles are just lessons in disguise. When you encounter them, try to learn the lesson they have to teach you.

Get Out of Your Own Way

Some of the biggest obstacles women face when they start trying to become who they want to be are self-doubt, self-criticism, self-blame, self-deprecation, and self-pity. Many times we doubt what we are doing will succeed. We fill our heads with so much negativity that there isn't any room for any positive input. Women are often self-critical about both what we are thinking and what we are doing. We engage in negative "self talk", saying things like, "My nose is too long." "My voice is too nasal." Or, "I'm no good in math." When you constantly criticize yourself for the way you look, what you say, and how you act, you are using self-criticism to convince yourself that you are unacceptable and not worthy of having your heart's desire. Women also tend to blame themselves for everything that goes wrong, not only in their own lives, but also in the lives of the people closest to them – like their friends and family. You need to realize that you can't be responsible for anyone else but yourself. Of course when your children are young, you teach them right from wrong, and how to be respectful of others, etc., but ultimately, when they grow up and make their own decisions, you shouldn't hold yourself responsible for how their lives turn out. You can only guide them on their way and hope for the best. As women, we often torture ourselves with regrets. We think of what we should have said or done and feel badly that we didn't handle the situation differently. We think to ourselves: "Why did I say that? I should have told my mother I loved her. I should have been more patient with her and listened better to what she was saying." We have to let go of the past and give ourselves a break, realizing that we did the best we could with the circumstances we had to work with at the time.

We can also get into trouble when we compare our lives to others. You make think that your single photographer friend who gets to travel to exotic locations and meet glamorous people has a better life than you, especially when your child or husband frustrates you. But you don't know what your friend is experiencing. Maybe she feels lonely and unfilled with her life, and is actually jealous of the stability of your family life. People so often envy others for what they don't have – gorgeous hair, a fun job, more money – and neglect to be grateful for all the blessings in their own lives. Take a moment right now to count your blessings. Consider things like your health, your family, having enough food to eat, etc. I suggest you do this gratefulness exercise the first thing every morning to get your day started in a positive way. It's also a great thing to do whenever you're feeling jealous about someone else's life. Possibly, one of the worst things a woman can do to undermine herself is to be self-deprecating. Even when you do a good job, you make excuses for how you could have done better, or you belittle yourself. There could be many reasons why you engage in this type of behavior. It could be old tapes from your childhood, where a parent or someone else who was close to you constantly criticized you, giving you negative input and making you feel like you were never good enough. Being self-deprecating can also be a way for you to get attention and positive feedback from others. By vocalizing your insecurities, you can get others to say nice things about you in an effort to counteract negative comments like: "I'm not pretty; I don't have any talent; I'm not special."

You may feel this way sometimes, but remember what I said earlier, you have to find a way to replace these negative thoughts with more positive ones. The truth is that all people have unique talents that make them special, gifts that are given to them to share with others. When you deny your gifts and talents, it is a dishonor to your spirit.

Akin to being self-deprecating is having self-pity. Feeling sorry for yourself won't do you any good, and can often drive people away from you because they don't want to be around you. You know you have self-pity when you are feeling helpless or hopeless about your life. You think you got a bad rap or a bum deal because of some of the things that have happened to you. Maybe your parents died and you had to live in foster care; maybe you were fired from your job; maybe your husband left you for another woman. While all these situations can be devastating, you have to find a way to move past them. Maybe you need to go to counseling or find a support group, but you must move on so that these negative occurrences don't ruin the rest of your life. When feeling self-pity, you are thinking small and dishonoring yourself. If you recognize any of the above self-defeating behaviors are prevalent in you, then it is highly likely you could be suffering from a self-esteem issue. It is important that you take any action necessary to transform your Self-Negatives by first understanding why you are feeling the way you do, and next, by taking action to change your behavior to reflect more positive thoughts and actions. True freedom comes from how you respond to life, and not from what life does to you.

Turning It Around

"The true believer begins with herself."— Berber Proverle

If you really believe that nothing good ever happens to you, and you affirm that either by saying or thinking it, then you have created a powerful universal force that can make failure your reality. However, changing your thoughts by first believing in yourself and that good things can and will happen to you, will make a difference. Say and think positive things everyday, and you call those same universal forces into your life to work for you in a good way. You may just be surprised to find how much better your life becomes by just thinking positively instead of negatively. You can condition who you are by changing your self-talk and remaking yourself from the inside out. Your mind creates your experience of reality, so learn to make your mind your friend instead of your enemy by thinking and saying nice things about yourself daily. Whatever we're saying about ourselves that isn't positive has to stop. Of course we're not perfect, and there are things we need to work on, but remember the Serenity Prayer: "Accept the things you cannot change, have the courage to change the things you can, and the wisdom to know the difference."

Answer the following questions:

1. Are you happy with yourself? Why or why not?

2. What would you change about yourself?

3. What are your positive characteristics?

4. What steps can you take today to make changes for the better?

5. Do you love yourself? Why or why not?

No matter what your past was like – whether you had a good or bad childhood – you still have the power to change your internal tapes and become more positive about who you are. Stop believing you don't deserve to have everything you want in life... because you do. In fact, you deserve everything life has to offer. You must find a way to love yourself (and that includes everything about you) before you can achieve your dreams. By "Self-Love", I'm not talking about being conceited, or self-involved, or self-righteous. What I'm talking about is a genuine caring for yourself and wanting the best for yourself – just as you want the best for the other special people in your life – like your friends and family. You've got to take care of yourself first before you can take care of anyone else.

You, yourself, as much as anybody in the entire universe,
deserve your love and affection. — Buddha

You can't give things that you don't have to give, and you have to start with yourself first. Take good care of yourself. Get enough rest; eat things you enjoy that are healthy for you; do some type of exercise you enjoy; and take time to have fun. Also, make sure the work you choose is work that you like. Life is too short to be stuck in a job you hate.

The Road Ahead

Where do you go from here? What's next for you? First of all, you should be aware that living in fear will steal your aliveness, so you have to make your courage bigger than your fear. So, don't be afraid to make some changes in your life. Since change is inevitable and going to happen with or without your permission, take control of the changes you want to make in your life. Take the first step. Make just one change. Perhaps you will enroll in a college course related to the field you would like to pursue, or perhaps you will just change your attitude to a more positive one. A positive mind and attitude promotes self-confidence. Whatever you do, make it your life purpose to grow into the best human being you can be.

As we search for meaning in our lives, the most important relationship we will ever have is the one we have with ourselves. There's only one me and only one you. We see the world differently; we think and act differently. Loving ourselves may be one of the hardest things we ever learn to do. But before we can give true honest love to others, we must first love ourselves.

Now is your time to shine and let the real you show. Learn from your past mistakes. Find out what works for you and let the rest go. Listen to your heart and take care of yourself. It's time to release any fear of failure, go ahead and envision your success. Be your own best friend, trust yourself, take control of your life, and be the best person you can be. Love yourself enough to do what is best for you by achieving your goals and daring to live your dreams......ON YOUR WAY TO BECOMING THE WOMAN YOU WANT TO BE! "I wish you great success."

Recommended Reading

Make Your Creative Dreams Real by Susan Ariel Rainbow Kennedy

Secrets About Life Every Woman Should Know by Barbara De Angelis, PHD

The Power of Resilience by Robert Brooks, PH.D. and Sam Goldstein, PH.D.

ABOUT THE AUTHOR

PAMELA COWAN

Pamela Cowan is the owner of a financial planning practice, Cowan Financial, LLC. Her key focus when working with clients is to educate and assist them in making better decisions in their lives especially as it relates to their finances.

Ms. Cowan is a graduate of the University of Toronto with a Bachelor of Commerce degree in Finance and Economics and a minor in Political Science. She has many years of experience as an accountant and later as a consultant in the computer software field which included international travel. In addition, she has conducted training for adults in accounting and computer applications. Her passion for teaching, led her to a career as a planner to be better able to assist and teach people on a more personal level.

Contact
Cowan Financial, LLC
2041 Stockmeyer Blvd.
Westland, MI   48186
(734) 722-5227
Pamela.A.Cowan@gmail.com

TWENTY-TWO

FINANCIAL SAVVY AND OVERCOMING DEBT

By Pamela Cowan

Overcoming obstacles, transition, and change is an appropriate title for a book directed towards women. We go through many different transitions in life; you start out, perhaps leaving home to attend college, get your first real job, setup your first apartment, marry, and then often may be back on your own, this time with children. If the marriage lasted (or you are on your second or third husband), most often the husband dies before the wife. The average age of widowhood is **fifty-six!** Women will outlive their spouses by seven years.

Okay, so what's the point? The point is that you need to be able to pay the bills and keep your savings and investments going, no matter what life may throw at you. You might need to pick up the pieces several times in your life, and especially when it comes to finances. At times, I think we handle our finances like our cars. Dad will look after it when we live at home, and then your husband or boyfriend takes over later.

I've picked a couple of topics related to finances that I think are essential. None of the information is new, nor is it intended to be comprehensive. A comprehensive plan can only be determined by a licensed professional who has the training and proper tools to correctly advise you. As planners, we find it amazing that the general American population has no problem paying a hundred dollars a month for various cable TV programs, but will not spend the five hundred dollars, on average, that it costs for a financial plan to determine if they are on track for retirement, or will be able to send their kids to college. Hopefully, some of the subjects I discuss will prompt you to seek more information, or to realize that there is a time and place to pay for advice.

Change is not always bad. One of my favorite quotes is by Carl Jung. "For better to come, good must step aside." We know that change will happen, and with it comes a level of stress. Having a handle on your finances and being adequately prepared can reduce the stress. Many times in your life the change is going to directly involve your money, such as a job loss, divorce, death or disability, so having some tools in your kit bag can help you address the money obstacles, get through the transition, and look forward to a new set of circumstances.

Organize

Much of the stress and concerns related to bill paying can be reduced by organization alone. Set aside a place in your home, no matter how small (maybe a drawer), that is specifically for collecting your mail and bills. When you pick up your mail, deposit the bills in the drawer. After you have run around the house tending to dinner, children, and whatever, you can come back to the drawer and tend to bill paying. Nothing will ruin your credit score faster than perpetually paying bills late, and if you are running around the house picking up scattered mail here and there, it is bound to happen. Being late will cost you higher interest rates on everything from credit cards to car loans and mortgages. We all have bills. If you enjoy having electricity and water at your home, chances are you are going to need to pay some bills.

Let's assume first that you do not use an electronic bill pay system, nor are you using the Internet for banking. In this case, you are going to need a good old-fashioned calendar to record due dates if you are unable to pay the bill as it arrives. Allow ample time for checks to arrive before the due date, if mailing them. If you have a computer at home, think about using online banking capabilities, which is provided by most banks, and is often free. Paying online avoids the increasing cost of mail, lets you select the day a payment will be removed from your account, and therefore allows your money to remain longer in an interest bearing checking account. Once payments are entered, the actual transaction between your bank and the utility company, for example, happens electronically. You need only setup the payment to be removed a couple of days prior to the due date. If all of this seems beyond you, go slowly. Pick one bill or vendor and try it. All connections with a bank occur over a secured line, and they will never ask you for social security numbers over the Internet.

Plan

Write down your goals. It is hard to go somewhere new without a map; it's even worse to wander through life without direction. Planning is different than budgeting. Planning is the overall view, your direction, what it is you want to do, to be and later, become. We all need to be looking to the future, even if saving for retirement is your only current goal. Having written goals will bring clarity and purpose to your thinking, and better direct your actions related to money. On some level, most people realize that writing out their goals not only commits them to thoughts and consciousness, but also communicates those goals to the universe.

As most planning guides suggest, you should set short and long term goals such as one year, five year etc., and make them specific. This is great advice because, without actionable or measurable targets, your goal is just a wish. "I wish I were wealthy and had no credit card debt." Does this sound familiar? A more effective approach would be to open a new account and save a small amount starting this week, and to prepare a list of the amount of money you have on credit cards as a first step toward making a plan to pay them off. We'll discuss more details on tackling your credit card debt later.

Your goals will change. You don't want the same things at age twenty-five as you will at sixty-five. This is an ongoing process. Planning is for the long-term with short-term benefits. What gets you there? Usually, a change in your thinking, and therefore your attitude, and a budget!

Budget

Most people without a budget, or who do not track their spending, underestimate what it actually costs them to live on a month-to-month basis. It is common for people to live their lives with their heads in the proverbial sand, lamenting their lack of money at the end of the month, and how they are unable to plan special vacations or other activities. Others refuse to budget because they feel it will infringe upon their style, and they don't want to be limited to spending a particular sum of money. On the contrary, budgeting, or at least writing down what you earn or receive as income, and listing your expenses will bring awareness to your situation, and give you the freedom without guilt to indulge yourself within your means.

Every successful business creates a plan and budget for what they intend to sell, spend, and invest in. Not only do they create budgets, usually a year in advance, but they also review them frequently to see how they are doing, and where they have deviated from the plan. If sales are down this month or this quarter, they can make adjustments to their spending so that they are able to remain in 'the black' or profitable, and stay in business. Okay, so how does this relate to you?

You need to keep your family and yourself in 'the black'. I have yet to meet a person who has not benefited from this exercise. We want to be clear about what we are spending, or at least what it is costing you to live month-to-month. In addition, with this information you can determine an adequate emergency fund so that you are able to handle unexpected expenses and gauge a realistic amount to save for retirement, such that your standard of living does not drop substantially when you are no longer earning an income.

Let's get started!

Exercise

You will need to list all of your sources of income. We are going to need to look at your net take home pay (the amount after taxes and your regular deductions). If you are not paid monthly or twice a month, take the annual amount and divide by 12. Then list all of the costs associated with your living expenses, which would include items such as housing, food, family haircuts and pet grooming. You will probably need to dig out receipts for the last year, as certain expenses fluctuate based on the season. You can use an average for items such as heating, cooling etc. Next, you need to include all items that do not get paid monthly. You will need to adjust these, so if you pay auto insurance twice a year, add the total and divide by 12 to get the monthly allocation. Finally, there are the items that you don't think about as living expenses. Do you send the kids to camp each year, go on a family vacation, buy birthday gifts, Christmas gifts etc.? How many times a month do you eat out? You will need to include these, also. Add up the expenses and subtract from the income. Surprised? Most people are. With this information, you can see if you need to make adjustments somewhere. Maybe you didn't realize that you were spending $300.00 a month eating out. It's not wrong, but when you see it, you can make changes toward goals that have more meaning for you, like increasing the education fund and having take-out one night, instead.

Let's make one final point before leaving this topic. You can see now what it costs you on average to live for one month, even though you do not pay each expense each month. It is important to plan on having at least three months of income saved, in case of an unexpected expense or job loss. If there is only one income earner in your household, double that amount. This money does not have to be sitting in a bank account where the interest you can earn is low, but it does need to be easily accessible so that you could get your hands on it, if needed. Many know how devastating a sudden job loss or similar event can be without adequate financial reserves. Budgeting, and the steps listed above, can help mitigate those hard times.

Saving and Investing

By now, hopefully, the importance of saving is coming through loud and clear, not only because you have read this chapter, but because you are also being deluged in the media with this message. Saving for retirement is a crucial element of your financial plans, as there are real concerns about Social Security and the rising cost of health care for seniors. I don't intend to go into a detailed explanation about all of the methods that you can use to save effectively. Instead, I will describe methods used for saving inside those financial instruments, and one of the issues that plague us as women.

First the good news, women are generally better investors. Why? Because we are less susceptible to locker room chat and don't run out and buy the latest hot tip. Statistically, people who stay in the market tend to do better than day traders, or people who jump in and out trying to 'time the market'. Now the bad news, women are generally more conservative, conservative to a fault, and this costs us. We pat ourselves on the back for having money in a savings account or 'safely' in bonds, which might be earning 3-4 %. Thanks to inflation, assuming a rate of 2%, you're actually earning real growth of 1%. With that kind of growth, how long do you think your money will last when you are drawing on it to live, especially when, not if, inflation increases? We need to save and invest more aggressively, but also safely.

One method we can utilize is to invest or save using mutual funds. A mutual fund is a method of purchasing a small part of many firms all at once. In this way, the investment involves less risk, and we can better reap the benefits of a particular type of company. Visualize two windows. One is a large picture window, and the second is the same size, but composed of many smaller panes of glass. If a baseball is accidentally thrown through the windows, which would you rather replace? The one with smaller panes has only lost a small section. You haven't lost the one large sheet of glass, which represents the entire window. When investing in a mutual fund, which represents investments in a hundred or more different companies of similar type and size, we are not as concerned if one company goes out of business, or is bought by another, as our investment is spread over the entire number of holdings in the fund. For the average investor, this is perfect. They have a safer investment because the investment risk is spread across many businesses, and they are achieving much higher returns, even though there is some increased risk. This is why you will see mutual funds used within many of the saving vehicles such as 401k, 403b and IRAs, to name a few.

Hopefully, you can now clearly see that one method to save in a relatively safe investment with larger returns involves using a mutual fund, but what kind of mutual fund? Well, actually several, and that's what diversification is all about.

Look at figure # 1.

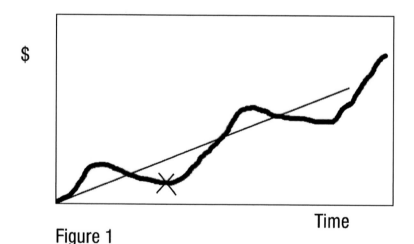

Figure 1

Here we are looking at the hypothetical return from one fund. It fluctuates with all of the changes that affect business and the economy. Let's assume that we need to make a major purchase at the time period marked with the small x. How are you going to feel when, not only do you need to spend a major portion of your savings, but it also needs to be withdrawn at a point when the market is at a low point for your type of investment. Not good. However, let's assume that you understand diversification, and you have an equal amount invested in a second sector.

Look at figure # 2.

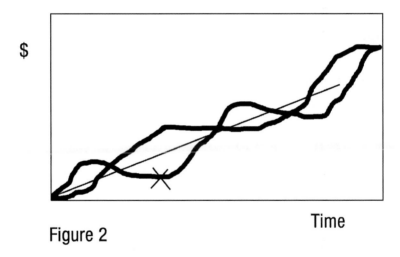

$

Time

Figure 2

Here we have two investments that work almost opposite to each other. At any given point in time, we can use money from whichever investment is at the higher return, and we have spread our risk by not having all our savings in one type of investment. On a simplified basis, that is exactly what savvy investors do, but we take it to a higher level of diversification. Although some mutual fund companies divide these sectors further, for ease, consider that there are 5 main segments or types named by their market capitalization or size and type of investment. The list is: Large Caps, Mid, Small, International and Bonds. The actual combination or percentage that you would use, in each sector, is normally determined by your risk tolerance. Most financial planners or firms selling financial products will have you take a small questionnaire to determine your risk level, and can therefore determine the appropriate percentages. I won't go into depth here, because my main point was to demonstrate the power of diversification, and even dividing your savings evenly among the five sectors would normally produce better returns than holding everything in cash or bonds.

Credit Cards and Debt

I love it when people tell me how bad credit cards are, as if they hop out of your wallet on their own and run around town collecting nasty balances. Credit cards are a wonderful tool. Like any tool, they can be abused, but usually they make much of our life a lot easier. Would you really want to carry several hundred dollars with you in cold hard cash to pay for a hotel room every time you traveled? But of course, there are pitfalls. Because we live in a cashless society, we have lost the sense of what we really spend in a weekend, on a spending spree, night out etc., which really brings us back to our earlier conversation about budgeting, reviewing and planning. We spend without planning, and just try and face the music when the bill comes in.

If, as you are reading this, you currently have substantial credit card debt, let's talk about a couple of strategies to address this situation and get you back on track. First, I would encourage you to seriously evaluate what happened. Don't make excuses, but be brutally honest. If no evaluation or true understanding takes place, history repeats itself.

Did you lose your job and suddenly overuse your credit cards for living expenses until you found a new job? When you had an argument with someone, have you felt better when you went shopping and overcharged to try to make yourself feel better? These are dangerous habits to get into. Taking charge of your finances goes hand in hand with taking charge of your life.

First, let's list all of the cards, their balances, interest rate, and each minimum payment. Also, make note of the credit limit on each card. In some instances, it may make sense to transfer a balance with a much higher rate to a card with a lower one. The overall debt will not drop, but it will not be growing as fast. Finally, add up all of the minimum payments per month. By now, you should have completed the budgeting exercise, so you will know how much money you are using to service credit card debt and what might be left over to help reduce this debt faster. Normally, it is advisable to pay down the card with the highest rate, but if you have a small balance on another card that you would be able to pay off within three months, you could tackle that one first. I find that the personal satisfaction gained by reducing the number of creditors, and the fact that you completely eliminate one from the list, will help your mental well-being, and help you to stick with the program. No matter which method you use, do not miss any minimum payments on any of the cards, or make any of your payments late. Not only will that affect your credit score as discussed earlier, but many cards can increase your interest rate for missed or late payments in addition to late fees. As you pay off each credit card, use the funds that were servicing that account and double up or increase the payments on the remaining cards.

The most difficult concept for people when paying down credit card debt is the idea that, unless the situation is dire (you can't even make the minimum payments), you should still be putting some money into your emergency fund. While this seems counterintuitive, without an adequate emergency fund, you have no place to turn for an unexpected expense, such as a car repair. Consequently, you will need to use your credit card and thus begins the vicious cycle. This unfortunately not only deepens your debt, but also makes the whole process seem like a losing battle. Last, but not least, don't beat yourself up. What's done is done. Take responsibility, make a plan to remedy the situation, and work the plan.

Make a list of credit cards, interest rates and balances:

Credit Card	Interest Rate	Balance
#1.		
#2.		
#3.		

I am convinced that taking these few steps will help you to feel more confident and in better control of your finances.

Recommended Reading

Smart Women Finish Rich: 9 Steps to Achieving Financial Security and Funding Your Dreams by David Bach

The Nine Steps to Financial Freedom by Suze Orman

Prince Charming Isn't Coming: How Women Get Smart About Money by Barbara Stanny

Secrets of Six-Figure Women: Surprising Strategies to Up Your Earnings and Change Your Life by Barbara Stanny

Notes:

_____

_____

_____

_____

_____

_____

_____

_____

_____

_____

_____

_____

_____

_____

_____

_____

_____

_____

_____

_____

_____

_____

ABOUT THE AUTHOR

ELIZABETH PALM

This chapter is for every woman. We all feel fear and worry. While it can be helpful at times, we need to tap into our resources and build our self-confidence. This chapter is about personal growth, expanding your comfort zone and finding your way without excessive worry and fear! Face your fears and do it anyway, you'll be glad you did!

Elizabeth Palm, President of Palm Consulting Group, is a Certified Professional Consultant located in Southeast Michigan. Ms. Palm has a degree in Business Management and is certified in Human Resources. Her expertise includes corporate training, human resource support, and business management. Ms. Palm is an active member of The Professional Woman Network and serves as a senior member on the PWN International Advisory Board.

Ms. Palm is highly knowledgeable on issues regarding customer service, human resources, diversity, self-improvement, women's issues and professionalism. Ms. Palm has conducted training in both formal and informal settings nationwide for thousands of corporate employees including executive management teams. Ms. Palm has a passion for sharing knowledge and guiding others on their journey toward success. Her presentations are interesting, insightful, and thought provoking.

Ms. Palm is also a co-author for several additional titles in the PWN Library and available on Amazon.com. such as:
- Customer Service & Professionalism for Women
- The Young Woman's Guide for Personal Success
- Overcoming the Super Woman Syndrome
- You're on Stage! Image, Etiquette, Branding & Style
- Women's Journey to Wellness: Mind, Body & Spirit

Ms. Palm is available as a keynote speaker, seminar leader, and consultant for groups, organizations or associations on a local, national and international basis.

Contact
Palm Consulting Group
PMB 343
19186 Fort St.
Riverview, MI 48193
(734) 282-8442
www.protrain.net

TWENTY-THREE

FACE YOUR FEAR!

By Elizabeth Palm

When you think of those subjects you dread talking about in your life, is fear one of them? Admitting or expressing our fears out loud seems to be one of those taboo subjects women don't want to discuss. It's like casting yourself in a bad movie. Yet, we all experience fear or anxiety at some time in our lives. Fear protects you when a potentially harmful situation arises. This emotion works as an internal warning system. It sounds an alarm that tells you, "Danger, move now!" If you start to step out into traffic, unaware of impending danger, I guarantee the person standing next to you, out of fear for your safety, will stop you or shout out a warning. Yet, in everyday situations, it is unlikely the person across the room would tell you they are paralyzed with fear at the thought of speaking up in a meeting.

When was the last time you had a conversation about fear? Do you ever express your fear? (I asked a few women these questions on condition that they would not be mentioned by name.) One thought talking about her fear was a sign of weakness, another thought that admitting she was afraid or anxious about anything made her vulnerable, and one woman believed she would never get promoted if she told her boss she was afraid to perform a particular task related to her job. "I'd rather lie or make something up than tell her I'm afraid to speak in public."

Fear, by any other name, can cause you to be confused, hesitant, or indecisive. Perhaps it is not fear but uncertainty of the unknown that paralyzes you. How do you handle your fear? Do you find other names to disguise it? Fear has many descriptions. How many of these do you recognize: anxiety, uneasiness, nervousness, dread, apprehension, concern, trepidation, angst and stress. Fear is a feeling, an emotion we experience, much like joy or happiness. Let's take a few minutes to talk about it. Let's take a look at what your fears are and balance them with options. Let's opt out of fear and into joy and release!

Understanding Your Fears

First, it's important to acknowledge that having some fear in life is normal. It affects everyone and is not specific to race, status, authority, or age. Fear creates limits, sounds like self-doubt, and can paralyze the best of us. And, fear comes to us at different levels. For instance, we could say the fear of mortality is a rather high level fear; the fear of not having enough is more of a moderate fear for some, whereas the fear of being late is not the biggest fear we would ever experience, but it could cause some form of discomfort.

Understanding what drives your fears or creates them is an important key to eliminating or reducing them. The tough part is putting it into words. Let's open the door to adventure and tackle a couple of your fears by first identifying them. What are your top three fears? (We won't tackle the mortality issue here, start small.) Write them here, in no particular order, just whatever comes to mind:

My top three fears:

1. _____

2. _____

3. _____

Now that the hard part is over, let's put a little perspective on each of these fears. For example, let's say you have a fear of speaking in public or to groups of people; where do you think that comes from? What are you really saying? Maybe it's a fear of saying the wrong thing, or maybe you are afraid someone will disagree with you and you won't know how to answer them. Is that possible? Of course it is. Speaking in public is the number one fear of 80% of the population.

What you need to understand is what *drives* that fear. Is it a lack of confidence, low self-esteem, or fear of rejection? Are you afraid of what someone might think? Or, maybe it's an experience you had that you never want to experience again. Anything is possible. Go back to your list and write down what you really think is driving those fears.

Roses, by any other name, still have thorns. You just have to take a different approach when dealing with them. You would not stop admiring their beauty just because of the thorns, right? You would find a way to eliminate them, or maybe wear gloves while working with them. Much like your fears, you don't want to dismiss them without first knowing how they came to be and the best way to handle them.

External Messaging

Every day we hear positive and negative messages. Sometimes the message generates a fear we would not normally have felt or thought.

On occasion, the message will tap into our memory and we will link this message to an old experience. The experience itself is not the key, but we *associate* the fear we felt that stops us in our tracks. I call these wet blanket messages. You've heard it before, just prior to the moment you take on a particular task the blanket is cast out: "This is hard, you won't be able to do it", "That color is bad on you" or "Don't even try, it won't work". It's like a wet blanket; the message is heavy, doubtful and negative. You stop just long enough to recall a time when you felt doubtful, and fear steps in to join doubtful, you hesitate, and the moment is gone. Has that ever happened to you? Did you turn around and decide you wouldn't do it because of the message preceding your action? Can you push yourself past the negative message? It takes some practice! You have to take that message and put a positive spin on it. Prepare yourself with an alternate, more positive message. List three wet blanket messages you've heard and write your positive alternative thought:

Wet Blanket Message:_____

Positive Response: _____

Wet Blanket Message:_____

Positive Response: _____

Wet Blanket Message:_____

Positive Response: _____

It is important to remember this experience is not the same as the "old referenced fear" you experienced. Believe you will have a positive experience regardless of the wet blanket message you may have heard.

The Worry Factor

Are you prone to spending countless hours worrying? Do your friends and family say you worry too much? Do you worry about little things constantly? Or do you imagine major tragedies will occur the minute you walk out the door? How many times have you found yourself lying in bed wide awake because you can't stop worrying about something? It's incredible, the minute your head hits the pillow the worry messages begin scrolling across the ceiling like an electronic message sign.

Like fear, there are times when worrying is helpful. It forces you to look at situations differently, and may even help you avoid some problems. For example, worry or fear in anticipation of injury is what caused someone to create airbags for our vehicles, or those little plastic plugs for electrical outlets that protect little ones from harm. So, some fear and worry have their rightful place in our lives.

It's the constant or unnecessary worrying that locks you in the house on a beautiful day. Worry can interfere with your ability to solve some problems, and can be very disruptive to your life. You've heard the saying, "Don't make something out of nothing." Worry and fear tend to be just that! I have found that 90% of what people worry about never even happens. It causes chaos and stirs up other emotions, but it seldom comes to fruition. So, what can you do about it? Here are some ways you can reduce your level of worry:

1. **Do a Reality Check:** If worry has its hold on you, then stop whatever you are doing and ask yourself some questions that will bring you back to reality. For example: Is anyone in any immediate danger? What specifically am I worried about? What about this situation makes me uncomfortable?

2. **Shift your Focus:** If you seem particularly focused on one event, shift your thoughts to some other activity. For example, if you are worried that you will be late to an interview tomorrow, shift your thoughts to what you can do to prepare yourself for the event. Have everything you need in one place. Put your keys, purse, and planner together, then you won't spend anytime looking for it in the morning.

3. **Stop Fanning the Flames:** Don't fuel your worry by getting other people to worry with you. Ask someone you trust if they believe your situation to be concerning. Avoid enflaming your worry by causing concern for someone else. For example: Don't tell your neighbor you are worried about her house catching fire if there is no obvious sign that would happen.

4. **Check your Perception Level:** Don't judge a book by its cover; it may be a very good read. When you make a snap judgment based on something you see, it can cause you to worry unnecessarily. For example: One woman, new in her neighborhood, saw a man in her neighbor's backyard. She immediately called the police because she thought he was going to break in. She never looked to see if her neighbor was home, or that this could be a family member. It turned out the man was her neighbor's brother; he was looking for potential problems in the roof.

5. **Listen to your Thoughts:** Does your inner voice or your thoughts seem to be running rampant and fast? Quiet your thoughts by focusing on your breathing, and stop those random, worrisome thoughts. Take three deep breaths, hold each one in as you count to 10 slowly, and then breathe out slowly as you count to 10, again.

6. **Do Something, NOW:** If your worry seems out of control, remove yourself from the situation and take a walk. Most times, if you start a consistent exercise routine, you won't have half the worry issues you have today.

7. **Talk to Someone:** If you believe your worry is legitimate, then talk to someone about it. Get another perspective on the situation by asking a friend or family member for their input and thoughts on the situation. If, at any time you feel you cannot control your worry, and you are completely uncomfortable, then it may be time to contact a professional for guidance.

8. **Change Your Worry to Curiosity:** Have you ever watched a four-year-old when they are introduced to a new toy? Most will look on with curiosity; they immediately want to know how it works, or what makes it special and different. Be curious about new events or activities. Engage yourself in curiosity; find out what makes it different.

Confidence and Courage

You're options are unlimited! All it takes is courage and confidence. Sounds easy doesn't it? That's because it is. Tap into your potential by believing you can overcome any obstacle in your path. Yes, it takes practice and effort. Move into it with all your energy and you will soon build momentum. Your friends will look at you with amazement first, and then they will want to know your secret. How is it that you are so confident? Where do you get the courage? Here are some ideas to get you started:

- Evaluate your beliefs. Write three things you believe strongly about yourself!

_____

_____

_____

- Surround yourself with positive people. Write the names of three people you know are supportive of you!

_____

_____

_____

- Boost your knowledge. Write three sources you can tap into that will increase your knowledge.

_____

_____

_____

• Own it! Take responsibility for how you think and feel! Write three ways you can do this.

_____

_____

_____

Your resources are endless. Use the Internet or the library to find material that will help you in your quest to be confident and build your courage in any situation.

Step Our of Your Comfort Zone

Take a chance, risk being different. If you want to grow, you must step out of your comfort zone and risk learning something new about yourself. It's difficult to be adventurous if you never leave the neighborhood. There are times when you are going to make a wrong turn; however, you might find it to be the best wrong turn you ever made. You may find yourself in the wrong place at the right time.

Start small and build your momentum. For instance, what if you wanted to travel to someplace you've never been, but you can't remember the last time you traveled and you can't find anyone to go with you? Start by deciding where you want to go, do your research and investigate the area. Check with a travel agent and find out the safest way to get there. Book it; make your reservations and go! If you're not sure of a fun place to go on your own, try Disneyland. It can be a very rewarding experience. The next time you take a trip, plan to explore the area you're in. You can always call a local travel agent or look the area up on the Internet. Explore and allow yourself to be curious enough to try something new. Create a meaningful experience for yourself.

What can you do today that will put you outside your comfort zone? Let's say public speaking is difficult for you. What if you took a class in Presentation Management? What doors would this one action open for you? List three activities or actions you can take to help you step out of your comfort zone:

1. _____

2. _____

3. _____

Now, take a few minutes and just imagine all the possibilities that could occur if you took these actions. Go beyond the obvious and write three possible, positive outcomes from each action you wrote. So, if you took a cooking class, is it possible you could become a chef? Why not? It won't happen over night, but anything is possible. Why not give it a try. Push past your fear and do it anyway!

Do It Anyway!

Here is my personal favorite method for overcoming fear: I put myself in situations where I am forced to deal with it. For instance, I used to be afraid of flying, tunnels of any kind caused me to feel trapped, and speaking in front of others was unnerving. How did I overcome the fears? I found work and hobbies that put me in every situation. I disliked but stayed with it until I overcame my fear. Most of the time, I forgot my fears because I was having fun, or enjoyed the experience so much I couldn't remember what I was afraid of!

For example, I took a job that required travel; nothing extensive, but it did require me to fly every six to eight weeks. I found reading to be particularly helpful during take-offs. Why? It forced me to concentrate on something other than my nervousness. My eyes were glued to the page, and I read slowly and purposefully. I accepted that I was not in control. I put my faith and belief in the fact that a higher power wanted me to overcome this fear. I said a prayer before every flight, expressing my thanks and gratitude for the blessing of safety and inner peace I felt as I traveled. I am now very comfortable flying. I look for the light at the end of every tunnel as if it was my highest goal, and I love speaking to groups of any size.

What can you do? Take a few minutes to look at your options. Consider where you would be if you never learned to drive. Imagine what you could do if you could eliminate your fears and do it anyway! What three things would you do if you had no fear to contend with?

I would: _____

I would: _____

I would: _____

You can have as much fun with this as you choose; however, I must warn you that, if you have too much fun, you might find yourself doing something different and exciting with no end in sight!

Additional Reading References:

Awaken the Giant Within, by Anthony J. Robbins

The Seven Habits of Highly Effective People by Stephen R. Covey

Chicken Soup for the Unsinkable Soul by Jack Canfield

ABOUT THE AUTHOR

ANDREA ALSTON-BRUNDAGE

Andrea Alston-Brundage is the founder and president of Zola Solutions, a consulting business that offers workshops relating to women's wellness. Andrea has developed, presented and participated in a self-esteem program for adolescent girls. Her interest is in motivating and assisting women in developing and achieving a balanced lifestyle. Andrea's ability to influence and motivate women has changed the way they live. She believes that building the spirit will help achieve balance and harmony in ones life. Andrea is also a certified school psychologist in the state of New Jersey. She works part time for a local counseling service. Andrea works for the Department of Defense as a business analyst in Philadelphia, PA. She is a member of Delta Sigma Theta Sorority, Inc. Andrea has been active in many community organizations and strives to be an active agent of constructive social change.

Andrea is currently working on her PhD, in clinical psychology, at Walden University. She received a Master's of Arts in school psychology from Rowan University, MA in Administration from Central Michigan University, a certificate in Mortuary Science from Mercer County College, and holds a Bachelors of Arts in Urban Studies/Health Management from Rutgers University. Her favorite scripture is Philippians 4:13, *I can do all thing through Christ who strengtheneth me.*

Contact
Zola Solutions
zolasolutions@verizon.net

TWENTY-FOUR

SAYING GOODBYE: DEALING WITH DEATH AND GRIEF

By Andrea Alston-Brundage

The Initial Loss

At one time or another everyone will mourn the loss of a loved one. This chapter is a result of a life-altering event, the death of my spouse. I didn't expect to lose my husband of ten years. When I said my wedding vows, I made a promise to be with him forever, till death do us part. Ironically, it was just that, until death. The entire process of his death was truly the most traumatic event I had ever experienced. The death of my spouse had a significant impact on my life. I experienced emotional, mental and physical upheaval from the time he was diagnosed with bile duct cancer to this very day, three years later. When my husband passed, I couldn't think or speak coherently. I experienced Elizabeth Kubler-Ross' five stages of grief: **shock, denial, anger, depression**, and **acceptance** first-hand. I became anesthetized after the loss. I drove twenty miles from the hospital to my home, alone at 3:00 am. Even though he had been ill for eighteen months, his death was unbearable. The shock provided insulation from the full blow of the loss. It allowed me to go through the necessary steps to make arrangements for the funeral and to get through the day after the loss.

I experienced denial after the shock wore off. It was a temporary defense and was eventually replaced with acceptance. I isolated myself from friends and family for a while because I was so angry, which made it harder for me to face the reality of my husband's death. When the denial occurred, it was below my consciousness. Prior to my husband's death, he was in the hospital for a month. I visited him daily. When he passed, I often thought he was still in the hospital. This emotion was a protective response to my husband's death. This stage assisted me in retreating from reality in order to face the death. Writing and seeing the obituary in the newspaper and seeing him in the casket helped bring his death into reality.

I felt rage and resentment. I often asked, "Why did this happen to me?" "Why am I left alone?" "Why didn't God take someone else who was not as kind, or someone who did not contribute as much to society as he?" I was so angry. I needed to be away from others. I had to take a leave from my job for three months. I couldn't bear being there. I was afraid that if someone said the wrong thing, I would snap. Anger was displaced onto those who were closest to me. I felt anger towards my husband not upholding his end of the bargain. Something so meaningful had been taken away, I felt resentful toward anyone related to my loss.

When I no longer denied the reality of the death of my spouse, numbness and anger were replaced with a great sense of loss. It was during this time I thought that no one else had experienced a greater loss than I did. I began feeling depressed and isolated. I couldn't concentrate and I slept very little. I was extremely fatigued, easily irritated, and short-tempered. My feelings of emptiness were exacerbated, and I looked at life as though it was meaningless. I felt truly detached from my surroundings.

Acceptance was the hardest stage for me to reach. It took between eight to ten months for me to accept the loss of my husband. Regression occurred constantly. However, the truth was recognized and would allow for healing to occur during this grieving process. I often wondered what was wrong with me. Why couldn't I get beyond this point? I seemed to do well for a while, and then start crying for no apparent reason, or become angry or resentful.

After some time, I had the tendency to idealize my late husband, even to the point of "sanctification". I would forget about the negative things that had happened during the marriage and selectively think of the good memories. It caused a great deal of guilt, as I was virtually putting my husband on a pedestal. This caused "survivors remorse", which I dealt with for many months. Don't get me wrong. My husband was a good man. However, in any marriage you have conflicts. After his death I wouldn't think about those things. When you lose your husband, you feel like your heart is breaking into tiny pieces. You lose your confidant, friend, lover, and security. You always feel vulnerable. The pain is so great at times that you just can't imagine ever getting over it.

When my husband was alive, we talked about the end. He was very concerned about leaving me. I tried to reassure him that I would be okay. I had waited until I was thirty-one to get married. I had lived on my own (the single life) six years prior to marriage. I tried to comfort him by telling him I would be all right. Little did I know that being alone post-marriage is nothing compared to pre-marriage? It's very difficult trying to fit into a life that you didn't choose. The friends that you had as a couple aren't the same friends you had as a single person. The friends that became your friends while you were a couple are no longer friends as a widow. Most of the people who said that they would call and keep in touch stopped doing so shortly after the funeral. You find yourself starting from scratch, building new relationships. However, you're not very comfortable meeting new people or opening up to them. To sum it up...No, I'm not okay. No I'm not living the way I thought I would be at this stage of my life, and no *I'm not over it.* However, I am accepting it. *I'm still standing.*

Surviving—Mind, Body & Spirit

Researchers believe widowed individuals have a higher morbidity and mortality rate than those who are married. After the loss of my husband, I went to LA Weight Loss so I wouldn't gain fifteen pounds. I lost fifteen pounds instead, which helped me feel better about myself. I started an exercise regime and ate healthier. It is so easy at a time like this to feel bad about yourself and have a low self-image. If you are an emotional eater like me, you will eat when you're depressed or stressed. I remember going to the super market one day and only picking up items that made me feel better (comfort food). I was so low. I didn't think about the consequences of my actions until all of the junk food was gone.

A few months had passed and I realized that I needed to see my family physician and have a physical, a mammogram, and my vision checked. I had been neglecting myself for 18 months. It was time for me to take care of myself. I made all of the necessary appointments and kept them. Everything appeared to be okay. I started taking yoga once a week, and it was wonderful. I was working on my mind and body. It was a very long journey, and I am still on my way to recovery. *I'm still standing.*

Generally speaking, women are less negatively affected by widowhood than men, possibly because they form relationships with other women. Friendships are vitally important after the loss of a spouse. Men don't often communicate as much with their friends. They may play basketball or golf, but won't talk about their feelings. Communication is very important when dealing with grief and loss.

I experienced many challenges after losing my husband and going through the grieving process. I relinquished my role as a wife and had to form a new identity. I had to assume control of my life again. I had to start taking care of myself. I had to learn to forgive again. Most importantly, I searched for meaning and had renewed hope. When trying to get back into a normal routine, I had to deal with many issues (e.g., enduring anniversaries, accepting responsibility and living for myself, focusing, reaching out and understanding). I realized my social network was affected. I was well aware that my social network played a significant role in my emotional health.

Social networks (new and old) provided support and companionship that was previously provided by my husband. I realized that some of the friends that I had prior to my marriage had relocated, and I was not able to reconnect. I was trying to replace and fill the void of losing my husband. The substitute relationships compensated for the lost relationship in terms of restoring my psychological well-being. I looked to other women for the missing support and companionship.

I found journaling to be very therapeutic. I discovered the art of journaling when I was a child. I could say things in my journal that I may not feel comfortable saying to another person. I found comfort writing down my feelings. Saying the words in writing was almost as meaningful as having a one-on-one conversation with someone, except you don't get a response. Going back to read comments I made was very emotional. When keeping a journal, you have to be sure that it is in a place only you would have access. If you want your information to be confidential, you cannot leave your journal accessible to others, as you run the risk of hurting someone's feelings if it is available for someone to read. Take it from me. Another lesson I wished I hadn't learned first-hand.

Early on after the loss, I looked for a grief support program. One was not available for close to three months, and when an opening was available, I attended weekly meetings. Everyone there had experienced a loss of a spouse. They may have lost a loved one 18 months earlier, or a month earlier. However, we all had something in common: the loss of a spouse. This was the best thing I could have done. Before I went to the meetings, I thought that I was the only one who had experienced such a tragic loss. After hearing and sharing what losses my new associates were dealing with, I could no longer look at myself as being special. There were others who had been married for longer periods, had children, or experienced sudden losses. One person went to work and didn't make it back home to say goodbye. I was able to count my blessings. My husband placed a phone call to me earlier in the day, before he passed, to tell me how much he loved me. Basically, he was saying goodbye to me, and I didn't realize it at the time.

Seeking help when you need it is one of the most important steps when dealing with loss. Knowing that there are other people who are experiencing similar things and are willing to share with you, you realize you are not alone. You are not alone on this journey. Even though your friends and family want to help you to get over the obstacles and provide support, it's not quite the same as sharing with someone who has been there. Often times your friends and family who are offering the support are also trying to tell you how to grieve, telling you it's been long enough. You should try doing things, like meeting people and being active. They don't quite get it. While attending bereavement counseling with your group, you are able to cry together, laugh together, and realize your situation may not be the worst. For eight weeks you are sharing your deepest and most painful feelings and your darkest moments. All of this is helping you through the necessary process of moving forward. I remember meeting a woman who lost her husband three months before the meeting. She had taken her life back and decided that she was going to drive to Arizona and Florida alone. Her goal was to go to Canyon Ranch (the ultimate spa resort). Anyone who knows me knows that I love a great spa resort. I would jump at the chance to visit a spa. But could I do that? Could I just get up and go like that? There was a time in my life that I would have done it without hesitation. I just didn't have the strength to do a road trip like that, especially not alone. But, then I realized this woman was probably a longtime housewife who only knew her life as a couple. She had been married to her husband for decades, and she found the strength to take a road trip solo. This was my inspiration. Three months after I lost my husband, I decided that I was going to take a road trip. It was only going to be a 5-hour drive, but it was a road trip all the same. My parents didn't want me to travel alone, so they decided to be passengers and accompany me to one of my favorite places, Martha's Vineyard. It was very cathartic. It was a place that I had visited with my husband,

and that in itself made it a little more difficult. However, I got through it by thinking about the places we went and things we saw. It helped me to move forward.

Having faith is extremely important during the grieving process. I have been a Christian for over thirty years. I can't recall a time when I needed the Lord more. I had always trusted in Him. I try to trust in Him in every situation. This was one of those times when I didn't understand my situation, but I trusted Him to get me through. When you trust in God, you must accept His answer and be content with it (even when it's not the answer you want). I must respect Him and His decisions. I must realize He has my best interest at heart. I may not have gotten what I wanted, but I must let His will be done. God has, and always will, direct my steps. Ultimately, He is in control of my life, and I must learn to trust Him. I may die disappointed, but God knows what is best for me. My belief is in what the Bible says, "*All things work together for good when we love the Lord.*" (Romans 8:28).

As in the Old Testament, God took Moses and the Jews the long way to the Promised Land. He was preparing them to be stronger. I look at my life. The Lord is taking me through to prepare me to be stronger. I had to turn it all over to Him. Every situation needed to be given to Him. I needed to relax and start trusting in Him to handle things.

It's Not About Me

After looking for answers to the question "why", I turned to my faith and tried to accept what had occurred as part of God's plan. I sought religious guidance for God's mysterious plan. I watched Pastor Joel Osteen and Joyce Meyer regularly while I was home mourning. It wasn't until I read Rick Warren's "*A Purpose Driven Life*", that I realized that it is bigger than me. I had a purpose. There was something that I needed to do in life. I needed to make an impact. I decided to go back to school and work on my Ph.D. And I am now in my third year. I knew that I couldn't do it alone. It was and is my faith in God that helped me get up each day. It was the support of my family and God's grace that I have remained sane. A year after my husband's death, I went to visit a friend in Germany. It was an opportunity that I couldn't miss out on. Prior to going, I had been thinking about adopting a child. This would have been an opportunity for me to make a difference in someone's life. I was fairly certain I was going to do it before I traveled half way across the world. While I was in Germany, I realized how big the world really was, and how my contribution to a child could really make a lasting impact. The global awareness helped put that into perspective. I put in my paper work and waited for my state to deliver a child. It took more than one year before the paper work was processed and a beautiful, talented, and intelligent five year-old was delivered. My life was starting to fill up. It had a purpose. I began living the way I believe God wanted me to live. It is work in progress and I'm *still standing.*

Moving Forward

It has been three years. I still visit the cemetery every birthday, wedding anniversary, and the anniversary of my husband's death. I miss him and think of him daily. However, I'm crying less, able to think a little clearer, and it's beginning to be less painful. I thank God for helping me move forward. I thank Him for the journey, and for allowing me to realize He is not finished with me yet. I take a day at a time. Each day is a day to make a difference. Ben Stein said, "The only life worth living is the one helping others." This is what helps me get through my valley. I hope that it helps you move forward. Seek out something that will make you happy. Grieve for your loved one. Communicate your feelings to others. Open up and let others in. Find your inner peace. Escape! Take a road trip. Let the wind blow through your hair. It is an awesome feeling of freedom. Just remember not to run away. It doesn't solve anything. The problems and the pain will go with you, and it will be with you when you return. Don't make major decisions right away. You may live to regret it. Don't complicate things. Keep them simple and meaningful.

If I were asked what were the 10 things that got me through the valley, I would say...

- Faith in God, who gave me the strength to get through each day.

- Support from family and friends.

- Bereavement counseling.

- Get away - trip to Europe, the islands.

- Interests - I found something that I enjoyed to fill the empty space (continued education, started a business).

- Spa Days - messages, manicures, pedicures

- Having someone in my corner to act as my cheerleader.

- Make life matter (do something for others that makes a difference, e.g. tutor, mentor, foster parenting).

- Prayer

• Listening to the inner voice and the voice of my deceased spouse.

Lessons learned - Treat each day as if it were my last. Appreciate those who love me; tomorrow is not promised. Always be good to myself.

If you are ever faced with a loss, just remember that you are going to make it. There is so much greatness in you. When you allow your path to be directed, you can then be brought through the valley. *I'm still standing, and so can you! God Bless.*

ABOUT THE AUTHOR

ROSEMARY MEDEL

A City Planner for the last seventeen years in Southern California, Rosemary has worked for the cities of Huntington Beach, Cypress and Signal Hill. A Bachelor of Fine Arts degree with an emphasis in Environmental Design has prepared Ms. Medel for her current profession in Land Use Planning. She feels strongly about giving back to her community and has volunteered her Planning expertise to the community where she currently resides. Rosemary is a former Planning Commissioner for the City of La Habra where she assisted in guiding development during her three-year term. In addition to being a city planner, Rosemary is a Realtor, and is the owner and president of The Medel Professional Development Group. Her firm is committed to training and preparing its clients to develop their professional image through improved public speaking and presentation skills, developing self- confidence, and mentoring in professionalism. She is a co-author of *Overcoming Obstacles, Transition & Change, Women as Leaders, Beyond the Body! Developing Inner Beauty, Young Man's Guide for Personal Success, Emotional Wellness for Women and The Baby Boomer's Handbook for Women.*

Rosemary is a certified trainer in Woman's Issues and is an International Advisory Board member of The Professional Woman's Network. She is also a member of both The Professional Woman Network International Speakers Bureau and the National Organization of Female Executives. Rosemary is available for personal and professional coaching sessions.

Her most important role and accomplishment have been raising her two grown children Rosalie and Eli.

Contact
Rosemary Medel,
The Medel Professional Development Group
P.O. Box 2204
La Habra, CA 90632-2204
rosemedel@juno.com
www.protrain.net

TWENTY-FIVE

PARENTING CHALLENGES

By Rosemary Medel

Our perception of parenthood is largely based upon our own experience. Two parent households, single-parent households, raised by aunts and uncles or grandparents, could have been your journey. Regardless of our experience, we begin to develop a list of qualities that we would want to possess as a good parent some day. What was your home environment like? Did being raised in these surroundings cause you to begin to develop your list of qualities that the ideal parent would possess? Or did you imagine how life would be if only you had different parents?

An early memory of my childhood was going for a drive with my father in his beautiful blue convertible. I believe I was five years old at the time. I would love the open air, the sports car feel, and just being with him. One afternoon I went with him on a drive. We arrived at this woman's home, whom I had never met. For some reason, I was uncomfortable being there as they smiled at each other, laughed, and enjoyed their time together. I remembered going into her bathroom to cry because I did not want to be there. I wanted to go home, but was made to wait. I felt unprotected and unloved. When we finally arrived back home, my mother asked me where I had gone with my father. I was telling her about my time away from home, when my father walked in on our conversation. I felt terrible, as if I had revealed a great secret. They obviously had problems and placed me right in the middle of them. That would be the last ride in the blue convertible.

I was the oldest girl and the second oldest child of a family of three children at the time. Being the observer of many years of infidelity and heartache between my parents, my mother finally decided to divorce my father. As a child in this environment, I developed my own list of parental qualities I wanted to someday possess. My top five qualities are as follows:

1. Never put another person or thing before my child.

2. Always make my child feel loved and protected.

3. Be a person that a child can admire.

4. Live a life of integrity.

List the qualities that you would want to possess as a parent, or that you presently practice as a parent:

1. _____

2. _____

3. _____

4. _____

5. _____

Let us review your upbringing. Did being raised in your particular family influence your perception of parenthood?_____
_____

What were the character qualities that you admired in those who raised you?
_____
_____

Would you raise your child in the same manner as you were raised? _____

Based on your experiences as a child, would you ever want to be a parent? List why or why not:

1. _____
2. _____
3. _____
4. _____

While growing up in a challenging family may not make for an ideal childhood, there is a solution. **Aspire to be the parent you never had**! I have two grown children who are individuals with various talents, and their similar propensity for music. Because Rosalie and Eli are so different from each other (beyond gender and age differences), I raised them with the same core values, but different approaches. If you have children, reflect upon the ways you raised your children. Were each raised similarly, or differently?

It would be easy to blame those who raised us because of their shortcomings as parents; parenthood comes with no manual! What I have learned in life is that the greatest gift you could ever give yourself is to forgive those that *attempted* to raise you. **Yes, attempted!** I once heard in church that sometimes people are simply doing the best they can.

You probably do not want to become a parent carrying all that excess baggage around with you! However, if you do not resolve the pain and disappointment of being raised in your family, you will carry it with you into all your relationships. If you are a parent, your children need you to show up as an adult and not a wounded thirty-five year old child. So what happens if you do not address the parent-child issues that you may be carrying with you? You will hold on too tightly to your child, thinking this is how one displays love and devotion.

Let's create a list of what "Holding on too Tight" looks like:

- Wanting straight A's from your child because it reflects upon how good a parent you are.

- Wanting your child to be the great athlete you were, or aspired to be, because sports made you feel significant.

- Demanding that your child be accepted to the best colleges.

If you believe that your child's happiness is the most important job you have, after setting behavior boundaries, respect for others, and responsibility for their actions, then you have come to the realization that you are now the Teacher!

Your child is merely on loan to you. By this, I mean that your purpose as a parent is to prepare them to be in the world on their own. List the traits your child must possess in order to live out in the world on their own:

1. _____

2. _____

3. _____

4. _____

5. _____

So, what is the challenge of preparing them to be out there? Maybe organized sports would be a good teacher to instill the values of discipline, compassion, create a good work ethic, and develop working as a team member. Some lessons I believed my son learned while playing organized sports is that you cannot always win, and life is not always fair. Sometimes you must lose. When your child's team loses, perhaps our job as a parent is to put the loss into perspective. List the values that keep sports and life in perspective:

1. _____

2. _____

3. _____

4. _____

5. _____

In loss we find our values and we develop our character. These values are carried off the court, off the playing field, and off the course. As a teacher, you will soon find that you just do not have all the answers for the challenges your child will face. I was always concerned that I would step in too soon to physically and emotionally protect my children. If I stepped in too soon, they would not develop their own survival skills. My daughter would not have learned to speak up for herself as a strong, young woman. My son would not have developed negotiation skills to resolve issues on and off the court, rather than resort to violence. I would have held on too tightly. I would not have learned to let my children fall. I would not have learned that this life is their journey, not mine. I am merely the loving teacher, ready to extend my arms to hold them if they need me. (Or write a check!)

What social skills do you consider important for a young person to learn, in order to survive in our society:

- _____
- _____
- _____
- _____
- _____
- _____

What are the consequences if the skills you listed are not developed?

- _____
- _____
- _____
- _____
- _____

As a teacher, you are always observing your students. As a parent, you know every mood of your child. You know how their day went before they say a word. You, after all, have a sixth sense when it comes to your child. So, how do you keep your child away from drugs and violence? Prayer is always a good starting point. But the other is to be completely involved in their lives. How do you do this and still not hold on too tight? Know as many of their friends as possible. Invite them to your home to observe their behavior and values. (This is otherwise known as bringing them to your turf!) Go to as many of your child's events as possible to let them know they are loved, and what they do is important to you. Get involved with their school, so that the teachers know you, the students know you, and that all know you are there to indirectly protect your child. What other ways of involvement do you think can be undertaken?

- _____

- _____

- _____

As you can surmise, transitioning from a turbulent childhood to being a loving and strong parent is possible if you fight your own demons to get to the truth of parenthood.

Top ten reasons to be a great parent (on the lighter side):

1. Because you want to love someone.

2. They will someday afford to take you out to dinner and pay!

3. You and your child will enjoy each other more after they pass the teenage years!

4. You get to watch Charlie Brown holiday cartoons together.

5. You get to teach them all about how cool your music was as a teenager, and listen to the remixes of all your songs in their music!

6. You get to enjoy all their crazy friends, and see them grow up, too.

7. You get to go through their first heartbreak with them because they trust you enough to share it with you.

8. You get to see them excel in sports, life and love.

9. You get to teach them how to drive and get their drivers license. (FREEDOM!)

And the top reason is:

10. They call you MOM!

I wish you a blessed and happy life, enjoying being a parent or aunt or godmother to some amazing young people in your life!

Notes:

THE PROFESSIONAL WOMAN NETWORK
Training and Certification on Women's Issues

Linda Ellis Eastman, President & CEO of The Professional Woman Network, has trained and certified over two thousand individuals to start their own consulting/seminar business. Women from such countries as Brazil, Argentina, the Bahamas, Costa Rica, Bermuda, Nigeria, South Africa, Malaysia, and Mexico have attended trainings.

Topics for certification include:
• Diversity & Multiculturalism
• Women's Issues
• Women: A Journey to Wellness
• Save Our Youth
• Teen Image & Social Etiquette
• Leadership & Empowerment Skills for Youth
• Customer Service & Professionalism
• Marketing a Consulting Practice
• Professional Coaching
• Professional Presentation Skills

If you are interested in learning more about becoming certified or about starting your own consulting/seminar business contact:

The Professional Woman Network
P.O. Box 333
Prospect, KY 40059
(502) 566-9900
lindaeastman@prodigy.net
www.prowoman.net

The Professional Woman Network
Book Series

Becoming the Professional Woman
Customer Service & Professionalism for Women
Self-Esteem & Empowerment for Women
The Young Woman's Guide for Personal Success
The Christian Woman's Guide for Personal Success
Survival Skills for the African-American Woman
Overcoming the SuperWoman Syndrome
You're on Stage! Image, Etiquette, Branding & Style
Women's Journey to Wellness: Mind, Body & Spirit
A Woman's Survival Guide for Obstacles, Transition & Change

Forthcoming Books:
Women as Leaders: Strategies for Empowerment & Communication
Beyond the Body: Developing Inner Beauty
The Young Man's Guide for Personal Success
Emotional Wellness for Women Volume I
Emotional Wellness for Women Volume II
Emotional Wellness for Women Volume III
The Baby Boomer's Handbook for Women

These books will be available from the individual contributors, the publisher (www.prowoman.net), Amazon.com, and your local bookstore.